ΘA

On the previous page are the Greek characters *theta* and *alpha*. Theta is the first letter in the Greek name for God -- Θεός -- (pronounced theh-OSS). Alpha is the first letter in the Greek alphabet. These two characters together are a reminder to keep God first in everything. They are placed alone in the center of the first page to signify God's centrality – He alone is the center and source, and Is before all things. God stands alone and should occupy the central part of our thoughts and lives.

Κέφινος Πάυλος Στέφανος

# Realms of Glory

*Encountering God in the Last Days*

by
**Kevin Paul Stephen**
M.Div., M.Th., B.Th.

*Broken Bread Publishing*
www.brokenbreadpublishing.com

Copyright © 2005 by Kevin Paul Stephen
Registered in the USA

All rights reserved. No part of this book covered by the copyrights hereon may be reproduced or copied in any form or by any means – graphic, electronic, or mechanical, including photocopying, taping, or information storage and retrieval systems without the written permission of the author, except for quoting brief passages in a review.

Unless otherwise indicated, all quotations of Scripture are taken from the:
 English Standard Version (ESV) of the Holy Bible
 Copyright © 2002 Crossway Bibles

This first edition was published in 2005 and was printed in The United States of America

ISBN-13   978-0-9769464-1-6
ISBN-10   0-9769464-1-6

Front cover illustration has been used by permission. It is from a series of 35 illustrations by Pat Marvenko Smith © 1982, 1992, on the Book of Revelation available as art prints and visual teaching aids. Call 1-800-327-7330 or visit www.revelationillustrated.com

# Contents

*Acknowledgments* ............................................................. 7
*A Introduction* ................................................................ 9

**Chapter 1** ***First Contact*** .......................................... 11
    Deep into the cloud of glory

**Chapter 2** ***Thick Darkness*** ..................................... 21
    The dwelling place of God

**Chapter 3** ***The Face of God*** .................................... 31
    Can God be seen?

**Chapter 4** ***Manifestations*** ...................................... 41
    The ways and works of the Holy Spirit

**Chapter 5** ***In The Spirit*** ......................................... 57
    The anointing, gifts, and normal Christian life

**Chapter 6** ***Heavenly Places*** .................................... 75
    Exploring heavenly realms and visions

**Chapter 7** ***Come Up Here*** ...................................... 89
    Back into the glory and angelic visitation

**Chapter 8** ***Undone*** ................................................ 105
    Radical encounters and the wilderness

**Chapter 9** ***Changed*** .............................................. 119
    From glory to glory and its profound effects

**Chapter 10** ***Friend of God*** ..................................... 127
    Does He call you friend? / Getting to know Him

**Chapter 11** ***Preparation*** ........................................ 143
    How to become an empty vessel, ready for the glory

**Chapter 12** ***The Temple*** ........................................ 163
    Encountering Jesus, Holy Spirit and the Father

*Chapter 13* **The Ark** ............................................................. *173*
  Forerunners and the end-time servants of God

*Chapter 14* **In That Day** ..................................................... *193*
  The coming outpouring of glory and Christ's return

**Ω Conclusion** ...................................................... *213*

  *About the Author* ................................................... *215*

# Acknowledgements

Through their love, prayers and encouragement, a number of people have been invaluable during the writing of this book. Without their support I have little doubt that this would not be in your hands now. I also want to thank those who spent time and effort in reviewing the manuscript and offered thoughtful and candid comments.

To Barbara Allen, Michele Hendry, Kevin and Stacey Yerian, Lisa Griess, Paula Stern, and Patrick and Jode Ferons: thank you. May God return the love you have given me and reward you many times over for your prayers, faithfulness, honesty and support.

In spite of his busy schedule and the many demands and responsibilities he faithfully meets, my pastor took the time required to offer careful and wise counsel as part of his review of this book. His keen insight and godly advice have helped to shape the final draft in no small way. Pastor Peter Young is a humble servant of the Lord whose guidance and friendship I cherish. Thank you, Peter, and may God richly bless you beyond what you have ever imagined. Get ready for the glory!

There is, however, one person who has been by far the most influential and valuable to me in all that went into writing this book. Countless hours of counsel, prayer, encouragement, proof-reading, and listening to me process and preach the message of this book, are just some of what she has given to me so freely. Without the many years of love, prayer, encouragement and selfless sacrifice that my wonderful wife has blessed me with, this book would have never been conceived in my heart. For all of this, and most of all for giving yourself to me, thank you, Patti. I thank God for you and love you dearly. This is for you.

# A
# §
# Introduction

The topic of the glory of God has captured the imagination of Christians in these days like never before. The saints of God are about to witness and participate in the most spectacular display of the Lord's power and character on Earth since the beginning of time. The knowledge of the glory of God will fill the Earth before the end of this age.[1] What is coming will bring both immense blessing to those who are prepared and severe punishment to those who are not. What do we need to understand about this and how should we prepare for what's ahead? What is the glory and are we ready for it? The answers may not be as apparent as they seem.

Though this is not an exhaustive study, nor a scholarly theological treatment of these subjects, I offer a presentation of the various supernatural ways God manifests, with a primary focus on the manifest glory of the Lord. Concise coverage is also found here on such topics as, the fire of God, His tangible anointing, the cloud of His presence, angelic visitation, the brilliant light that clothes Him, and the present day ministry of His Holy Spirit.

In 1986 I was struck by the power of God and left my mortal body to be taken into the thick darkness where the core of God Himself dwells.[2] The experience was terrifying and beautiful. Seventeen years passed before a similar trip into the glory of God brought greater understanding of it all. Yet, I still fail to grasp it entirely.

Until the writing of this book, I have revealed to only a few the details of these, and other, experiences I have had with the Lord. They are deeply personal and I have cherished them as something shared only with God. Recently He prompted me to describe portions of a few of my encounters with Him to help in drawing His beloved saints closer to Him in these last days.

---

[1] Hab 2:14
[2] Ps 97:2, 1 Ki 8:12

# Realms of Glory ☼ A - Introduction

While I believe that all Christians should have a vital and exciting spiritual life filled with supernatural experiences in God, I also believe that it is crucial to weigh and validate all spiritual experience with the testimony and teaching of the Holy Scriptures. It seems that often either sound doctrine and theology are forsaken for the pursuit of spiritual experience, or the inverse. We should come into greater revelation, relationship and experience with God by way of both. The Bible points to an experiential relationship with the Lord and all spiritual experience and revelation can be measured against the written Word for validation. The two were never meant to be divorced, and we are in the time when the Lord will reunite them in wholeness. Not in the sense of the "Word camp" and the "Spirit camp" coming together in unity, but by the two finding their fullest expression together in individual people.

I have endeavored to substantiate both the experiences I relate, and the theological basis for the ideas I put forth here with careful examination of Scripture. Though not all will agree with every point made, I trust that my brethren will chose to maintain the bond of peace in Christ while holding their own views.

Relationship is built upon shared experiences. It continues to be my primary goal to progressively know God and experience all of His glorious attributes and manifestations. As my friendship with God has developed, He has been gracious to reveal more about His glory, character and various manifestations. Through theological study, visions, supernatural experiences and in personal conversation with Him, I continue to grow in my knowledge of God.

It is my pleasure to share some of these things with you here. My desire is that the Lord might use this in some way to make Himself known in greater depth to you and draw you further into a growing intimate friendship with Him. I hope this book gives you a greater appreciation of God's marvelous character and better prepares you to explore the many realms of His glory.

Kevin Paul Stephen
May 2005

# Chapter 1

§

# First Contact

Thirteen years had passed since my first extreme encounter with God. Sitting in an Ira Kellman meeting in Denver Colorado, my mind went back to the day of my baptism at age ten. Something in the atmosphere was reminiscent of that day when I heard the Lord's audible voice. It made me long to hear Him again with such clarity. The atmosphere was charged with God's presence and the anticipation of those in attendance was palpable.

Ira's meetings were anything but dull. Often God would surprise everyone with spectacular displays of His power. The anointing and power that the Lord released through Ira was extraordinary. New Year's Eve was an especially supernatural event for those who came to see Ira. It became an annual tradition in the mid and late 1980s. Many of us who knew Ira found it hard to understand why the Lord kept him relatively hidden, considering the high level of gifting and anointing he was endowed with. But we didn't complain as it allowed for personal relationship with him and we were blessed to partake of his ministry in a more intimate way. With only thirty or so people present at this particular meeting, all who desired to receive personal ministry and experience the Lord's presence and power were certain to have the opportunity.

Some people would come out of curiosity after hearing reports of the healings and unusual outpouring of the Holy Spirit that followed Ira wherever he went. Others came hungry for God or desperate for physical and emotional healing. Skeptics would show up at times determined to confirm their judgments that it was all emotional hype.

Those who approached the presence of God that manifested around Ira in humility and reverent fear were blessed as God touched them. Conversely, those who challenged the prophet or flippantly approached the glory around Him were touched by God's power in another way. Often the consequences were severe. It was apparent that God took it as a personal affront to treat Ira Kellman with disrespect. Whatever the motive for coming to see Ira, few left in the condition they arrived in.

In my heart I was crying out to God and asking for more of Him. I knew there was more and I wanted it. I wanted to see Him, to hear Him, to experience Him like never before. I had already been pinned to the floor for hours in a state of unconscious blissful peace during meetings earlier in the week. Holy laughter overcame me and persisted until I thought I had broken ribs. I was stumbling around in a spiritual drunken stupor, but it wasn't enough. I was calling out to God in my spirit:

> "Lord, please let me see You. I want to see and experience the core of who You are. I want to know the person that emanates all of this wonderful peace, power, joy, prophecy and healing. This is great, and I'm really enjoying all of it, but I want to see the source, not just experience the manifestations of Your power."

I sensed that I really had no idea what I was asking for and that it would likely kill me, should my petition be granted. These impressions were about to be confirmed. I was under holy fear having seen the results of asking amiss or with impure motive while around Ira. Even so I prayed:

> "Lord, let me have all of You I can take. Let me come as close to You as I can possibly stand. Pull the trigger on me, Lord – I'm desperate to see You!"

My thoughts were so caught up in these things that I really had no idea what Ira was preaching about or what was going on around me in the meeting at the time.

I sensed the Lord say to me "Well, all right."

Just then my mind was brought back into the meeting as I heard Ira's voice.

"Kevin, come up here." I staggered forward and stood before him.
"What do you want from God?" Ira asked.

The question shook me as it seemed that both it and the answer were reflected in Ira's piercing gaze. I felt he was testing me and that somehow saying that I wanted to see God and wanted more than He had already given me was not a good answer. I also didn't want to sound stupid in front of the other people there. So, I mumbled something like:

"Well, I could use some direction on a few things right now and......"

Ira nodded and grinned. I could see in his face that the Lord had told Him what I really wanted. He interrupted the pitiful attempt to conceal my true desire with "Uh-huh" and motioned with his hand toward my chest. What happened next shocked everyone there, and none more than me.
It felt like a wrecking ball struck my chest and sent me sailing several feet backwards before I landed on my back. I remember hearing several people gasp as I hit the floor. I don't recall making contact with the carpet as my entire being was enveloped in an intense nerve-numbing energy. All strength and control fled my body. My ears felt plugged and were ringing, my lips were buzzing. Ira's voice seemed far off as I heard him chuckle "He's OK. Don't touch him."
The ringing in my ears reached a crescendo ending in a bone-jolting "pop". Then there was absolute silence. I lost all awareness of my body, and my senses were suddenly and strangely altered. The remainder of this segment of my experience was completely void of sound. Whatever happened in the meeting room after that moment escaped my awareness.
A thick cloud of gray smoke and sparkling light encased me. All sense of time, direction, and space vanished. Something...no,

someone was drawing me deep into the cloud. Though direction and space were meaningless, there seemed to be a core, or center, that this cloud obscured. The sensations of paralysis and rapid travel were only eclipsed by an increasing vibration that reverberated throughout my being. The power that surrounded me was beyond imagination and was intensifying as I passed deeper into the fog. Billows of dark gray smoke speckled with fiery bursts of light buffeted me in supercharged waves. Fear and panic gripped me. I was completely naked, transparent and helpless as I raced toward the Source - the immediate presence of God.

I was certain that the rapidly increasing power surging through me would bring annihilation if it continued. My sinful state blared in vivid contrast to the absolute purity, awesome power and holiness that took on substance all around me. It was tangible and increasing in density. I was not at all prepared for this.

Communication with God in this state happens instantaneously and largely without words. He sees everything all at once and nothing can be hidden from Him. I could feel His attention squarely focused on me and there was no escaping His gaze. I was frantically confessing and repenting of everything I could think of, including things I had never done. I shuddered while blurting out questions and cries for mercy.

"Am I going to die, Lord? Am I dead now? Oh God, what a stupid idea to ask for this. I'm sorry. Really! Please don't destroy me. Are you going to let me into heaven? Is this heaven? Please, let me stop here and let's talk this over before I get blown apart."

The only answer that came back was:
"I've got you. You're not going to die now. Try to relax."

"Relax?! Yeah, OK. I guess that means I'm forgiven. That's good. Maybe I'll make it through this after all" my mind raced.

Turning away from the extreme raw immediacy of His power, majesty and presence was impossible. He just was, and He was everywhere around me. In awestruck fearful response my innermost being involuntarily spewed forth worship in recognition of His remarkable attributes. "Holy" was the only word possible in natural language. It was pitifully inadequate for the magnitude of what I was being exposed to. And then the question came:

"Is this close enough?" I realized that I was no longer traveling and the level of penetrating energy around me became static, though no less intense.

"Yes! Thank you, Lord," I shouted back in gratitude.
"Well, if He were going to destroy me or do something really painful He probably would have done it by now," I reasoned. "I better do my best to obey whatever He tells me – this is NOT the place where you want to mess up! I'll never complain about not having my prayers answered again, if I survive this. OK, He said relax…. so take a deep breath," I coached myself.

I don't know if it would be accurate to call it breathing, but I inhaled deeply the thick glory that held me fast. It was fantastic. It felt fresh and cool. The fragrance was subtle and sweet. Filled with life and pure energy, it began to cleanse me inwardly. I continued to draw in the glimmering dark mist and tried to still myself to hear what the Lord would say next.

Still quaking in fear, I then became aware of God's indescribable love for me. Though I deserved hell and the severest of judgments, God's wrath was stayed by the cocoon of acceptance and love that caressed me. It seemed the balance between wrath and love, justice and mercy was tipped toward my salvation as my spirit offered praise and thanksgiving to Jesus.

Revelation began to flow as I started to relax. Though my sins had been forgiven the effects of sin and the root of iniquity remained within me. It was definitely good that the Lord allowed me to stop here as I was being cleansed and renewed. I didn't want to think what would happen if I were taken any closer to Him.

There was much work to be done to prepare me for my next meeting like this with Him. Many things would need to be done away with, and other things would need to take root. The working out of my repentance still needed to be done. It was all so obviously beyond my ability. For a moment I feared failure was inevitable, along with certain doom.

Then the realization came that what I needed to succeed in this, and all other things He would ever require of me, was available in that place. I was hopeful that He would grant me the opportunity to walk these things out as I was being washed in His presence.

As I became still before Him in speechless awe, the transfer of things beyond description began. No conscious thought could discern what I was receiving. Yet, I sensed that it was all to help me in completing the mission He had for me. Trust became no issue. The Lord's great kindness was now beyond doubt.

Some of the events and impressions I am describing did not happen in any particular order. Some of them happened simultaneously, and others seemed expanded in duration beyond the limits of comprehension. The experience was non-linear. I can only attempt to express it in temporal terms. All efforts to place certain aspects of the things I perceived in the eternal into sequential order will fail at some point. Natural language cannot adequately convey the totality of what happened. The duration of this portion of the encounter is impossible to accurately gauge in time. The eternal is beyond any unit of measure, but it seemed to last for half an hour or more.

Suddenly the awareness of time began to seep back into my consciousness. I knew that my encounter was about to take a shift, but not completely end. "One more deep breath of the glory" I thought as I tried to inhale. The atmosphere seemed to have become a vacuum as I was unable to draw in breath. A more deliberate attempt produced a long gasp that I heard with my natural ears. I felt my chest rise and a sharp tingling sensation over my entire body. Blood surged through my veins. Breathing became relaxed and easy.

I heard someone whisper, "Oh thank God, he's alive." And another "Is he OK?" I was unable to open my eyes or move for most of the remainder of the meeting. I still felt loosely tethered to my body as I drifted in and out of the room while continuing my

Gerald

Mauitoe

Jim

Drew

wordless conversation with God, enjoying the now euphoric serenity.

From people who witnessed this I understand that I lost all color of complexion upon landing on the floor and appeared to stop breathing for more than a minute or two. No one came near me or touched me during this time.

A few hours later I was able to sit in a chair without spilling onto the floor again. Someone who witnessed all this then asked me:

"Where did you go? I mean, it was pretty plain that you left here for awhile."

All I could manage was "I'm not sure. I was with God."

"Yeah? Well, you sure weren't here. You looked dead. That was pretty scary," she said.

"Yeah. Pretty scary," I mumbled.

Whether I actually "died" or not, I cannot say for certain. But I think it would be safe to rank it a close call. I was certainly away from my body for a time. It took several days to completely regain my physical strength and coordination.

There was so much about this experience that I didn't understand at the time, and some things I still don't. I had no doubt that I came close to death. If not for His great mercy you would not be reading this now. You can bet I'm more thankful than you are for that!

But what was the purpose of it all? Did He just decide to answer my foolish request and let me know just what I was really asking for? Was He trying to scare me, get a good laugh, teach me a lesson, let me know it wasn't a game to approach His glory, give me a gift, or dazzle me with His power and beauty? Yes, I think He wanted all of these things, and more, from it.

Everything was just great soaking in the anointing and enjoying the overwhelming power of His presence, drinking the new wine of His Spirit and feeding on the anointed preaching of His Word. But no, that wasn't good enough. I had to have more. Brilliant, huh?

So, how was it that I went from spiritual party town to holy terror town and vacated my body in nothing flat? What was the problem? It seemed like everything between the Lord and I was pretty good up to that point. What changed?

I was obviously unprepared for my visit with the Almighty. Surviving the glory requires a completely different approach and level of preparation than enjoying His other manifestations. As we will see, what most people call the glory of the Lord is really just a strong manifestation of His presence, or what some call the anointing. The glory is something altogether different.

Holy fire, new wine, and the wind of the Holy Spirit are really the activity and ministry of the person Holy Spirit. We will be looking at each of these manifestations and their purpose as we go along. Also, there are multiple levels and dimensions of glory. These are yet largely hidden from the saints living at the time of this writing. I believe that as you read on with a responsive heart toward God the Holy Spirit will reveal things beyond the words written here in preparation for you to venture into realms of glory yet unexplored.

Before we begin to explore the various topics concerning God's glory, let me say that by no means is what I write here meant to be an exhaustive study. It is not my intention to present these things as the fullness of revelation available or as a theological treatise on the subjects discussed. Also, please understand that as we seek to increase the revelation we have of God's character, His heart toward us, and the nature of His various manifestations and ministries, the goal is not to "put God in a box" to be studied. We should be careful not to limit our experience of God, nor our understanding of Him, by what we may come to know about Him through experience and theology.

There's plenty more to be discovered about God and His glory than any of us will come to grasp given eternity. That's exciting to me! Only God is the definitive authority on who He is. What we discover about Him should always lead us back to the Source of the hidden treasures of wisdom and revelation in the knowledge of Him held in trust as our inheritance. So, take whatever the Lord may reveal to you here and use it as a spring board to launch you into higher realms of discovery in His glory.

While God wants us to have extreme experiences with Him, all of our spiritual experiences should be carefully examined in the light of Scripture. Many people claim to have experiences where they are told or shown things that are in direct contradiction with the will and ways of God, as revealed in the Bible. We must insist that our experiences are in agreement with Scripture before accepting them as "authentic." I have seen many people get off track by insisting that what they "saw" or "heard" or otherwise sensed "in the spirit" was from God, even though it was in direct opposition to the written Word of God.

Some folks would insist that a spiritual experience is not from the Lord unless an exact account in Scripture can be found, where every aspect and detail is identical. I respectfully disagree with this assertion. When biblical characters had their experiences with the Lord there was no precedent for them, in many cases. While John's Revelation of Jesus Christ included symbols and visions of things that were seen by Ezekiel, most of the Revelation was unique to John's experience. Prophetic words are not limited to what is written in Scripture explicitly. However, all prophecy must agree with the sure prophecy of Scripture. Likewise, all authentic divinely inspired visions, dreams, and other spiritual experiences must be in agreement with the written witness of Scripture, though not limited in message or content to the written Word.

I will be presenting scriptural support for various aspects of the personal experiences written here. I hope this will help you in judging your own spiritual adventures, while illustrating a number of other points as well. You may want to refer back to chapter one at times to see how the things we consider compare with my first trip into the thick cloud of glory. I encourage you to evaluate all of the encounters I describe in this book with the witness of the Bible.

My motive for sharing these things with you is to bring greater understanding of our inheritance as Christians and to point the way to obtaining it. I believe that many of those who read this will have far greater encounters with God than these in the days ahead. The point is to glorify God above all else, and to spark a greater hunger in you for Him.

God asked me to write this book to help bring others into the deep realms of His glory. His desire is for you to come into closer relationship with Him and partake of the spiritual riches He has prepared for you.

In chapter seven I relate an experience with the Lord that occurred seventeen years after the one described in this chapter. In that encounter I again found myself in the thick gray cloud of glory and was taken even closer to Him. A series of extraordinary visions and angelic visitations occurred prior to and after that voyage into the cloud of His glory. The Lord lovingly led me through the preparation process prior to this second event, enabling me to more fully enjoy and benefit from it. I mention it here only to point out that in both of these episodes I was taken into the same dark cloud.

Before writing this book I had given partial accounts of these events to only a few people. Most of them posed this question as their first: "I thought God was light and when you were taken into His presence you saw a bright light. So, what's up with the clouds and darkness?" We'll find the answer as we consider the dwelling place of God.

**Activation**

I encourage you to agree with this prayer for you so that you might enter into greater realms of God's glory, even as you read this book. As you agree with this prayer, not only for you but for all who read this, I believe that the Lord will multiply the release of His Spirit and glory over your life.

*Lord, I ask You to open up the understanding of all who read this book, that they might access all of the spiritual riches that You have prepared for them. Help each one who meditates on the message of this book to encounter You in new ways and come to know You in greater depth. Father, even as Your sons and daughters read this book I ask that you open the heavens and pour out your Spirit upon them as you prepare them for greater realms of Your glory. I thank You for all that You have made available to us in Your Son, the Lord Jesus Christ. Amen.*

## Chapter 2
§

# Thick Darkness

Many people who have had near death experiences (NDEs) report seeing a being that shines with brilliant white light. We know that Satan can appear as an angel of light to deceive[3], which may account for some for these reports. However, some of these NDEs are very likely encounters with the Lord of Hosts. Those who have had heavenly experiences, such as trances and visions, also commonly describe God as radiating brilliant light. Scripture also supports this in numerous places, as it describes the Lord as being radiant. Let's examine a few passages that associate God with light.

John the Beloved tells us that God is light in his first epistle.

> *1 John 1:5*
> *This is the message we have heard from him and proclaim to you, that **God is light**, and in him is no darkness at all.*

The psalmist also had revelation of the light that emanates from God.

> *Ps 104:1-2*
> *Bless the LORD, O my soul!*
> *O LORD my God, you are very great!*
> *You are clothed with splendor and majesty,*
> ***covering yourself with light as with a garment***

Yet, a number of passages in the Bible tell us that the Lord of Glory also dwells in thick darkness, or a cloud.

---
[3] 2 Cor 11:14

*Ex 20:21*
*The people stood far off, while Moses drew near to **the thick darkness where God was.***

*Deut 5:22*
*"These words the LORD spoke to all your assembly at the mountain out of the midst of the fire, **the cloud, and the thick darkness**, with a loud voice; and he added no more."*

*1 Kings 8:12*
*Then Solomon said, **"The LORD has said that he would dwell in thick darkness..."***

*Ps 97:1-2*
*The LORD reigns, let the earth rejoice;*
*let the many coastlands be glad!*
***Clouds and thick darkness are all around him**;*
*righteousness and justice are the foundation of his throne.*

Thick darkness, as used in theses verses, describes the tangible glory that encapsulates God. This is His dwelling place, within the cloud of glory. At times it is described as smoke. Here are a few examples:

*Ex 19:18*
*Now Mount Sinai was wrapped in **smoke** because the LORD had descended on it in fire.*

*Isa 4:5*
*Then the LORD will create over the whole site of Mount Zion and over her assemblies a cloud by day, and **smoke** and the shining of a flaming fire by night; for over all the glory there will be a canopy.*

*Isa 6:3-4*
*..."Holy, holy, holy is the LORD of hosts;*
*the whole earth is full of his glory!"*

*And the foundations of the thresholds shook at the voice of him who called, and the **house was filled with smoke**.*

*Rev 15:8*
*and the sanctuary was filled **with smoke from the glory of God** and from his power,*

The Lord's glory is described as smoke in these verses. We can also see that great power accompanies the cloud and a response of fear and awe is evoked from all who see it. So, how do we reconcile the fact that God appears to be a being of light but also dwells in thick darkness?

Light is one physical manifestation of God's glory. Fire and smoke (or clouds) are also types of God's glory. We will find that these various forms of glory have unique purposes and are associated with specific members of the Godhead in later chapters.

Psalm 104:2 says that God covers Himself with light as a garment. So, light is not His substance, but only His garment, according to the psalmist.

However, John the Beloved said that God *is* light and in Him is no darkness at all. As we read the verses that follow, we begin to see the fuller context of what John is talking about.

*1 John 1:6-7*
*If we say we have fellowship with him while we walk in darkness, we lie and do not practice the truth. But if we walk in the light, as he is in the light, we have fellowship with one another, and the blood of Jesus his Son cleanses us from all sin.*

John is using light as a metaphor to describe the purity of eternal truth that is characteristic of God. We can see this as John contrasts light with darkness. Darkness is used here to symbolize a "lie," or the denial and absence of God's eternal truth. What John is saying in effect is "God is Truth and in Him is nothing contrary to Truth. If we do not practice the truth that He has given us consistently and without compromise, then we have denied it, or lied against the truth and therefore cannot come to know God in reality."

So, this passage has less to do with the radiant beauty of the Lord than it does with eternal truth, or light, of which God is the source.

What of the various manifestations where God appears as light throughout Scripture then? I believe that light is the garment, or outer visible substance, that He chooses to let us see at times. As glorious, pure and wonderful as this is to behold, His true innermost being is masked by the blinding radiance that shines forth from Him.

> *1 Tim 6:14-16*
> *to keep the commandment unstained and free from reproach until the appearing of our Lord Jesus Christ, which he will display at the proper time — he who is the blessed and only Sovereign, the King of kings and Lord of lords, who alone has immortality,* ***who dwells in unapproachable light, whom no one has ever seen or can see.***

This light is pure holy energy generated in His core. It is radiated substance, but it is not God in total. There is still more of Him hidden within the brilliant glorious light seen around Him. The transfiguration event of Jesus seen by three of His disciples illustrates this very well.

> *Matt 17:1-8*
> *And after six days Jesus took with him Peter and James, and John his brother, and led them up a high mountain by themselves. And he was transfigured before them, and his* ***face shone like the sun, and his clothes became white as light****. And behold, there appeared to them Moses and Elijah, talking with him. And Peter said to Jesus, "Lord, it is good that we are here. If you wish, I will make three tents here, one for you and one for Moses and one for Elijah." He was still speaking when,* ***behold, a bright cloud overshadowed them****, and a voice from the cloud said, "This is my beloved Son, with whom I am well pleased; listen to him." When the disciples heard this, they fell on their faces and were terrified. But Jesus came and touched them, saying, "Rise, and have no fear." And when they lifted up their eyes, they saw no one but Jesus only.*

The three parallel passages in the synoptic gospels that describe the "Mount of Transfiguration" event are rich in symbolism.[4] We could easily fill several chapters just exploring the riches locked up in these passages. I encourage you to study and meditate on these passages and go beyond what I cover here. I trust the Lord will reveal things of great eternal worth as you do.

In the transfiguration account we see both light and the cloud of glory manifest. First, Jesus is seen with Moses and Elijah. Elijah was a prophet of fire, while Moses spent time in the dark cloud of God's glory. The Lord granted Moses' request to see His glory there in the thick darkness. We see Jesus talking with them as He becomes radiant and His garments became brilliant.

Jesus is the physical expression of God; the natural representation of the Father. His glorification is seen as light here. Notice that the disciples were able to see and bear this sight. Peter was even able to speak, but seems to have been bewildered because of the magnitude of what was happening. It wasn't until the cloud of glory covered them that they fell on their faces in terror. The glory of the Father overshadowed them and was even more awesome than the brilliant splendor that radiated from Jesus.

The Lord reveals Himself outwardly and releases power, revelation, healing, prophecy, etc. in the form of light. God is seen on His throne as brilliant light and fire by John in Revelation chapter 4, and by Ezekiel in his throne room experience as well.[5] However, God conceals Himself in the thick darkness that surrounds Him.

All beings that see the light shining forth from God are completely overwhelmed with awe. The power that emanates from Him is beyond comprehension and impossible to resist. Nothing created could possibly stand to see what is concealed deep within His garments of majestic splendor. Even so, the cloud of His smoky glory is infinitely more powerful and awe inspiring.

How is it that He rules and releases immense power and authority in the form of light, but conceals Himself in smoky clouds? What makes the smoky glory so much more powerful and

---

[4] Mt 17:1-8, Mk 9:2-8, Lk 9:28-36
[5] Ez 1:26,27

awe inspiring? Why don't more people report seeing the thick darkness where God dwells? The answers to these questions will take us a long way in understanding the nature of God's glory, and God Himself, in greater depth.

Notice that Jesus did not take all of His disciples along to witness the transfiguration event. Only His three closest friends were invited. When Moses had his various experiences with God in the cloud of His glory, it was by invitation as well. The Lord commanded the rest of Israel to not even come near the mountain. Even when the Lord had the elders come up the mountain to eat with Him, He called Moses up higher, alone.

Does God play favorites? Well, yes and no. His desire is that all would come to know Him in a consummate way. However, He only allows His closest friends into the most intimate places with Him, close to the very core of who He is. So, the key question is: how do we become the friend of God? The bulk of this book is focused on answering that question. We will deal with it specifically in chapter ten.

The thick cloud is an even more intense manifestation of glory than light. It is the vapor that emanates from God's essence; His inner most being. The glory of light is the release of power, authority, revelation, knowledge of eternal truth, counsel, and so on. But the smoky glory is the substance of what makes God who He is. It is far more holy, powerful and personal than the other manifestations, as wonderful as they are.

Most of us don't expose our most private inner selves to others we don't know or trust. We may have friends and relatives that we love and trust to a degree, as we share our hopes and dreams with them. But only if we come to know our closest friends, or our spouse, and trust they will value, accept and keep private what we share of ourselves, will they be granted a view of our most intimate inner self. It is no different with God.

There is a place deep within each of us that is so personal and protected that only the Lord can touch it directly, if we allow Him to. His inner most being is so pure that He only reveals it to His closest friends; those who have allowed themselves to be prepared by Him. Limiting access to this place of exposure to His inner being is an act of mercy, as He is concerned with our survival.

Approaching His glory without the requisite level of preparation and proper attitude brings swift judgment and death.

The Lord's most intense pressing desire is to know us completely and make Himself known to us in the open exchange of self.

*Isa 30:18*
*And therefore the Lord [earnestly] waits [expecting, looking, and longing] to be gracious to you; and therefore He lifts Himself up, that He may have mercy on you and show loving-kindness to you. For the Lord is a God of justice. Blessed (happy, fortunate, to be envied) are all those who [earnestly] wait for Him, who expect and look and long for Him [for His victory, His favor, His love, His peace, His joy, and His matchless, unbroken companionship]*
*AMP*

Connection of our heart to God's at this point can only occur at the deepest spiritual level.

*Ps 42:7*
*Deep calls to deep*
*at the roar of your waterfalls;*
*all your breakers and your waves*
*have gone over me.*

I love this verse. It so fitly describes my travels into the thick darkness where I have the most intense, real personal exchange with the Lover of my soul. His glory overwhelms as waves of His love and the unfolding, continual revelation of His marvelous character cover and saturate. When the soul and flesh are silenced and cleansed through consistent subjection to the spirit, we are able to go beyond ourselves and find entrance into the deepest dwelling place of God. The most intimate exchange possible with the Lord occurs through unhindered connection between our inner most being and His.

*Ps 139:11-12*
*If I say, "Surely the darkness shall cover me,*
*and the light about me be night,"*
*even the darkness is not dark to you;*
*the night is bright as the day,*
*for darkness is as light with you.*

The many realms of His glory are secret places where He reveals the hidden treasures of wisdom and revelation in the knowledge of Him to a far greater degree than in other heavenly places.[6] Concealed deep within the cloud that covers His being are tremendous riches of truth and pure holy spiritual life and power. The cloud of His glory is one visible manifestation of this.

We will see in later chapters that wisdom, revelation, truth and spiritual blessings are available to all who are in Christ, in varying degrees and on different spiritual planes -- what Paul called "heavenly places." Within the thick darkness of His dwelling place are many realms and dimensions waiting to be discovered as well.[7]

*Prov 25:2-3*
*It is the glory of God to conceal things,*
*but the glory of kings is to search things out.*
*As the heavens for height, and the earth for depth,*
*so the heart of kings is unsearchable.*

God has concealed the greatest treasure of all in His glory. It is only given to kings to search out and discover them. Kings are those of noble character who have been granted the authority to rule, within specific boundaries. Although we are all called to rule and reign with Christ, kingship is not automatically granted to all in the Kingdom. What I mean is, not everyone will submit to Christ's Lordship to the degree required to rule as a king in His Kingdom (or in the earth) in reality. It is the desire of the Father's heart that we would all grow into a place of trusted stewardship, through the

---

[6] Eph 1:16-19
[7] In chapters five and six I will discuss these other realms of heaven.

refining of our character and motives, through obedience, and various processes of preparation.

However, obtaining our inheritance is conditional. We must obey the commands of God as given in Scripture and by the direction of the Holy Spirit.[8]

God clothes Himself in light and is pleased to show this to many, even though it cannot be approached. However, He dwells in thick darkness, hiding the most central part of His being in a cloud of glory. Only those who are summoned into the cloud will truly experience and see His glory, and come close to the very center of God. All true saints have access to the throne of God, just as Satan does.[9] Yet few have truly experienced His glory. That is about to change before long.

God is not trying to keep anyone at a distance, but we must be prepared in order to survive such intense encounters with Him. God freely gives us all things and loves us all intensely. Jesus has paid the price once for all to be able to enter into the process of salvation and come to know God in all of His fullness. All of this was initiated by God Himself, so we cannot earn what He chose to grant us by grace.

Yet there is a cost, and laying hold of all that He has made available to us by the completed redemptive work of Christ is contingent on our obedience. It is a free gift that costs everything. Are you willing to pay the price to see Him in His glory?

So, is it possible to see the core of God's being that is hidden within the thick darkness where He dwells? We will find the answer in the same way we come to know all truth -- by seeking the face of God.

**Activation**

If you are willing to pay the price to see the Lord's glory, then I encourage you to make this your prayer:

---

[8] Chapters 5, 6, 10, & 11 provide extensive support for these assertions
[9] Job 1:6

## Realms of Glory ☼ 2 - Thick Darkness

*Lord God, I ask You to reveal yourself to me in all Your glory. Father, show me the light of your splendor and the things hidden in the thick darkness where You dwell. Prepare me to meet You in the smoky cloud of Your glory. I love you and want to know you in the deepest way possible. All praise, honor and glory belong to You forever! Amen.*

# Chapter 3
## §

# The Face of God

God is spirit and cannot be seen. The substance of the Lord's essence is neither matter nor energy, though He is the source of all things created. What we are able to see in the form of His glory is not God Himself, but divine radiation from His Being.

*1 Tim 6:16*
*who alone has immortality, **who dwells in unapproachable light, whom no one has ever seen or can see.***

*John 1:18*
***No one has seen God at any time.** The only begotten Son, who is in the bosom of the Father, He has declared Him.*
*NKJV*

*1 John 4:12*
***No one has seen God at any time.** If we love one another, God abides in us, and His love has been perfected in us.*
*NKJV*

God told Moses that no man shall see His face and live.

*Ex 33:20-23*
*But," he said, "you cannot see my face, for man shall not see me and live." And the LORD said, "Behold, there is a place by me where you shall stand on the rock, and while my glory passes by I will put you in a cleft of the rock, and I will cover you with my hand until I have passed by. Then I will take*

*away my hand, and you shall see my back,* ***but my face shall not be seen."***

If God is spirit and therefore invisible, why would He say this at all? If His face cannot be seen, why would He say that one would not live if He were seen?

The face of a person is the most distinguishing part of their outward appearance. God the Father does not have a literal face. This is an anthropomorphism (ascribing human attributes to God) used to help us understand something about God's nature.

The Hebrew word and the Greek word used in the Septuagint for *"face"* here is used in the context of the most personal aspects of a person's form. So, what He is referring to is His most personal unique attributes. These are beyond direct examination in their entirety, and infinitely vast. The complete scope of what the *"face of God"* is cannot be fully known

We may come to know God in ever increasing depth through nature, direct conversation, divine revelation, the written and prophetic Word, and transfer of intimate knowledge through direct spiritual union with Him. However, these are all mere reflections of His primary essence.

*Rom 1:19-20*
*For what can be known about God is plain to them, because God has shown it to them. For his invisible attributes, namely, his eternal power and divine nature, have been clearly perceived, ever since the creation of the world, in the things that have been made*

Since God is the prime mover and self-existent Creator, then His invisible innermost self is the source of all things seen. So, we consist of a portion of His substance, as He breathed His life into Adam and we all come from Adam. Mankind is created in His image, yet we are individual beings -- separate persons from God.

Although we are made in His image, we are not exact duplicates of God. God is unseen, we are seen. We have a body of flesh made from the substance of the Earth. He does not (though He lived in one as Christ, before His Resurrection). Many of His attributes are incommunicable, or non-transferable, to us. Such as, His omnipotence (He is all powerful), self-existence (He is uncreated and eternal, without beginning or end), immutability (His character and essence never change in quality or magnitude, yet are infinite in depth), omniscience (God completely knows all that can be known), and omnipresence (He is always everywhere at once). God is separate from His creation, but His life fills it as He intersects all of heaven and the universe at every point. These paradoxes may help explain why we cannot see the "face" of God and live.

Spirit beings are eternal, as they were formed from the indestructible substance of God. The Hebrew word and the Greek word used in the Septuagint in Exodus 33:20[10] for *"live"* is not the same word used to indicate the natural life of a creature. It refers to the invigorating life that originates in God. It is the "breath of God," or His imparted essence. So, essentially the Lord told Moses that the very breath of God within man would cease to exist if man were to fully "see" God's face -- that is, to be made completely aware of all of His distinguishing features in their fullness. I believe that in order for us to "see the face of God," we would be directly exposed to the purest core of His incommunicable attributes. Let me explain further.

Our finite being would have to take on the complete depth of God's infinite Being in order to even begin to grasp what we would be trying to perceive. For example, to fully know what it means to know all things, we would have to know all things. To fully understand power and authority without end we would have to become omnipotent. To completely comprehend what it is to be from everlasting to everlasting, we would have to be self-existent. In other words, we would have to become exactly like God to be able to perceive His essence completely. This is impossible for anyone but God.

There are only a few things God can't do. He can't lie, He can't die, He can't contradict His own nature, and He can't create anything equal to or greater than Himself.

So, for us to *"see His face"* in the way that Moses desired to, we would have to take on the total of God's substance, which would

---

[10] *"for man shall not see me and **live**"*

be obliteration for us. We would have to become equal with God, which is impossible, as we just determined.

Even so, it is our "destiny" to come to progressively know Him as completely as possible. This is our inheritance. It is the mystery of Christ in us -- the hope of glory.[11]

But doesn't it also say that Moses spoke with God face to face? How do we explain that?

> *Ex 33:11*
> *Thus the LORD used to speak to Moses **face to face**, as a man speaks to his friend.*

To help understand this let's look at another verse, this one in the New Testament, that speaks of the same thing.

> *1 Cor 13:12*
> *For now we see in a mirror dimly, but **then face to face**. Now I know in part; then I shall know fully, even as I have been fully known.*

Paul used the Greek words *prosopon pros prosopon*[12] for *"face to face"* here. In his *"The Complete Word Study Dictionary of the New Testament,"* Spiro Zodhiates suggests the meaning of this phrase within its original context is *"with nothing intervening."* So, it would seem to suggest that when we pass into glory, there will be nothing to hinder our intimate direct experiential knowledge of the Lord. We will no longer be limited to the wispy glimpses of His Person we now enjoy on this side of eternity's veil. This is the same Greek phrase used in the Septuagint in Ex 33:11. However, this is not the same thing as *"seeing His face"* as used in Ex 33:20.

So, when God told Moses that no person could see His face and live, this does not have the same meaning as Moses speaking to God face to face. One carries the meaning of being completely exposed to all of God's incommunicable attributes in their fullness (which

---

[11] Col 1:26-27

[12] πρόσωπον πρός πρόσωπον

we have determined would mean annihilation), while the other phrase is descriptive of unhindered and clear communication.

After the great White Throne Judgment at the end of this age, all who have been given glorified, incorruptible, resurrected bodies, and have been wed to the Lord Jesus, will be able to behold more of the face of God than is possible in our current mortal state.

> *Rev 22:3-4*
> *No longer will there be anything accursed, but the throne of God and of the Lamb will be in it, and his servants will worship him.* ***They will see his face****, and his name will be on their foreheads.*

Those who keep the *"name"* (meaning the defining characteristics) of God in the forefront of their minds (*"on their foreheads"*), by meditating on His character and attributes in holy intimate communion, will be given a place in the most intense realm of His glory for all eternity. They will forever gaze into the wonderful "face" of the Almighty, and be completely immersed into perpetual and ever increasing revelation of His marvelous essence. They will be clothed in the Lord's glory as a garment, and forever show forth His radiant beauty.[13]

This will be made possible by the transforming work that lesser realms of glory and the ministry of the Holy Spirit have wrought in them. We become like the thing we focus on, and so these saints will take on the most complete likeness of the Lord by spending themselves to behold Him in His glory above all else.[14]

> *2 Cor 3:16-18*
> *But when one turns to the Lord, the veil is removed. Now the Lord is the Spirit, and where the Spirit of the Lord is, there is freedom. And we all,* ***with unveiled face, beholding the glory of the Lord, are being transformed into the same image from one degree of glory to another****. For this comes from the Lord who is the Spirit.*

---

[13] Rev 21:9-11
[14] 1 Jn 3:2-3

All of this explanation is essential to understanding the manifestations of the Lord's glory and its effects on whatever it touches. Exposure to the glory of God works sanctification in us and makes us ready for greater levels of glory. It transforms us into His image.[15] And as we found earlier, the more like God we are in character, essential quality and substance (that being holy and pure spirit) the more of His glory, or essence we will be able to endure, grasp, and absorb. What a wonderful cycle of escalating experience in God!

In many passages of Scripture we are admonished to seek God's face.[16] In fact this is the primary thing He requires from each of us. We were created to be dazzled by the infinite glorious attributes and wonders of God as He reveals them to us in loving kindness. It thrills His heart as we are dramatically affected and respond in love, thanksgiving and worship. Seeking His face is how we gain experiential knowledge of the Holy One. Of course, we can never completely *"see"* His face in fullness as we have already discussed, so this command to *"seek God's face"* refers to a continual quest to come to know God more completely.

Refusing to seek His face stirs up God's anger and is the root cause for the release of His judgment and wrath. To neglect this is an insult to Him as we fail to recognize His marvelous character and attributes and then respond in awe and worship. Failing to acknowledge His holy character and appreciate His desire to make Himself known to us in a personal way, is the first step toward falling away and being given over to a reprobate mind. If we neglect to seek Him above all else and adore Him in worship, we begin to lose the knowledge of God and put our eternal well being in jeopardy.[17]

Relationship is built upon shared experience. Many who claim the name of Christ know much about Him, but have little real experience with Him. It is not enough to know facts about Him, or to understand the doctrines of the Christian faith, or to memorize large portions of Scripture, or even to pray and read the Bible daily.

---

[15] 2 Cor 3:18
[16] 2 Chr 7:14, Hos 5:15, Ps 24:3-10
[17] Rom 1:18-29

We must pursue a real experiential relationship with Him where we seek to know Him intimately. Eternal life is found as we seek His face – to come to know His unique qualities in ever increasing depth. Our primary purpose is to know God, and to bring Him glory by making Him known to others.[18]

When Moses descended from Mt Sinai after spending time in the Lord's glory, his face shone with such intensity that the people would not come near him for fear.[19] The face of Moses was made radiant with the same glory that he had been exposed to in the thick cloud on the mountain of God.

We have seen that the face has the most unique identifying features of a person. When we spend time beholding the glory of God, we are changed into His likeness and He makes the unique identifying features that He put within us conspicuous and radiate the glory we have received. We can only fully fulfill the purpose of the unique individual will of God for our lives if we spend all to bask in His glory. As we let all that is contrary to His nature die so that we then take on His image, He is able to illuminate and empower our talents and gifts and release us into our unique purpose for making His glory known.

Others will become uncomfortable being around those who find this level of liberty and oneness with the Lord. The Lord's glory and purity upon one so changed and radiant exposes the darkness in others, and makes evident how far short of the glory they have fallen. It brings conviction and makes a response compulsory in those who come near it.

At times we must veil the level and intensity of the glory in which we may normally walk in order to reach those who would otherwise shun the message of hope that God so desires to touch them with. This is similar in concept to "becoming all things to all people in order to save some" and not allowing the spiritual liberty that we may enjoy to become a stumbling block to those who are seeking truth with a sincere heart.[20]

When we *"talk with God face to face"*, we remove the veil in order to allow for the most intimate relationship possible with Him.

---

[18] Jn 17:1-4
[19] Ex 34:29-35
[20] See 1 Cor 9:19-23, Rom 14:20-22.

We make ourselves vulnerable and present ourselves to Him without reservation or pretense. We can enjoy His beauty and take on the radiance of His glory, as we allow Christ in us to purify and use our God given gifts and talents to make Him known in reality to others.

We are able to experience the Lord's presence and receive His wonderful gifts, as we are baptized and filled with His Holy Spirit. The initial baptism, or total immersion experience, in the Holy Spirit is made available to us from the moment we first trust in Him, but must be received and acquired by faith.[21]

However, access to deeper revelation and realms of glory is progressive. Each heavenly experience or journey prepares us for adventures in higher realms. As we cooperate with His refining process, the Lord calls us up into these higher realms.

God is accelerating the maturation of our character in these days. He wants us to abide continually in His manifest presence and take up residence in His glory, not just sojourn into heavenly places.

While our transformation through the revealing of God's glory is the result of the work of the Holy Spirit[22], the glory itself is not the work or person of the Holy Spirit. Considering various supernatural manifestations will help us see how the glory differs in magnitude and purpose from the work, ministry and gifts of the Holy Spirit.

**Activation**

We can be assured that the Lord will answer the sincere prayers of those who love Him and desire to seek Him above all else. Make this your prayer and trust the Lord to reveal His most intimate attributes to you.

*Father, I desire to know You in the most intimate way possible. I thank You for creating me for close relationship with You and for liberally giving of Yourself to me. I thank You that You have freely given me all things in Your Son Jesus, who made the way for me to come to know Your most defining features. Lord, please grant me a*

---

[21] More on this in chapter five
[22] 2 Cor 3:15-18

*willing heart and the hunger to know You in ever increasing depth. I will seek Your face with my whole heart in joyful anticipation. Thank You, Holy Lord.*

# Chapter 4
§

# Manifestations

The Holy Spirit loves to make His presence and work known through various supernatural manifestations. However, the conspicuous presence of the Holy Spirit is not synonymous with the manifest glory of God.

Some of the ways the Holy Spirit manifests may seem unusual and surprise us at first. But we should be careful not to be offended by the ways He makes His power and presence known, nor make inaccurate judgments about things we may not fully understand. This has been the natural initial response by people since the outpouring on the Day of Pentecost as recorded in Acts chapter two.

The one hundred and twenty folks who had fire, power and the release of speaking in other tongues come upon them by the baptism of the Holy Spirit were accused of being drunk by those who came to see what the commotion was all about. I realize this isn't written in the record of Acts, but I imagine the folks in the upper room were probably staggering around laughing, the way some folks do today in renewal meetings. They were definitely under the influence of the Spirit. Good times!

The person Holy Spirit is sensitive and is easily grieved and offended. He will not remain where He is not loved, honored and welcomed. If we misjudge the ways He works, or mistake Him for an impersonal force rather than the wonderful person He is, we will grieve Him and risk missing out on coming to know Him better and enjoying the many great gifts He has for us. To help us please Him and make Him feel welcome, let's take a look at some of the manifestations of the Holy Spirit to get a better understanding of His ways.

## Rain

Throughout Scripture, rain symbolizes the blessing of the Lord upon His people.

> Joel 2:23
> "Be glad, O children of Zion,
> and rejoice in the LORD your God,
> for he has given the early rain for your vindication;
> he has poured down for you **abundant rain,**
> **the early and the latter rain,** as before."

We can see that these verses refer to an outpouring of God's Spirit, as we read on and find the fuller context of the passage.

> Joel 2:28-29
> And it shall come to pass afterward,
> that I will **pour out my Spirit on all flesh;**
> your sons and your daughters shall prophesy,
> your old men shall dream dreams,
> and your young men shall see visions.
> Even on the male and female servants
> in those days I will pour out my Spirit.

This prophecy found partial fulfillment on the Day of Pentecost and is finding its ultimate fulfillment in these days. We are in the time of the acceptable year of the Lord, just as Jesus announced when He quoted Isaiah in Luke 4:19. Rain is a sign of God's favor and blessing. We live in the age of grace when the Spirit of the Lord is working in the earth to draw all people to Him.

A supernatural manifestation of literal rain has been reported in various places around the world where the Holy Spirit is pouring Himself out upon those hungry for Him.

> Zech 10:1
> **Ask rain from the LORD in the season of the spring rain,**
> from the LORD who makes the storm clouds,
> and he will give them showers of rain,

*to everyone the vegetation in the field.*

*Isa 45:8*
*"Shower, O heavens, from above, and let **the clouds rain down righteousness;** let the earth open, that salvation and righteousness may bear fruit; let the earth cause them both to sprout; I the LORD have created it.*

This is the season for us to call out for God to rain down upon us in mercy. The rain of His Spirit comes to cleanse, and refresh. We need this type of outpouring to prepare us to hear the quiet whisper of His voice.

**Wind**

The sound of a mighty rushing wind was heard just prior to tongues of fire falling on the heads of the believers in the upper room. The wind of God's Spirit blows in power ahead of the fire to clear away loose debris, reducing the fuel that His holy fire will consume. This is an act of God's mercy. Wind is also associated with the clearing away of things contrary to the will of God, and causing storms that bring about correction to His children.

The wind of the Spirit can be heard and felt in gatherings of believers at times as well. I have personally felt the strong rush of the wind of God on a number of occasions.

*1 Kings 19:10-13*
*And he said, "Go out and stand on the mount before the LORD." And behold, the LORD passed by, and a great and strong wind tore the mountains and broke in pieces the rocks before the LORD, but the LORD was not in the wind. And after the wind an earthquake, but the LORD was not in the earthquake. And after the earthquake a fire, but the LORD was not in the fire. And after the fire the sound of a low whisper. And when Elijah heard it, he wrapped his face in his cloak and went out and stood at the entrance of the cave. And behold, there came a voice to him and said, "What are you doing here, Elijah?"*

Sometimes the Lord acts in mighty displays of power in order to clear the way for a more intimate encounter. Though the Lord sent the wind, earthquake and fire, He was not in them. We have often mistaken His works for His person. We miss the message for the manifestation. God uses the spectacular to get our attention at times, but He is found in the subtle. God is in the quiet whisper that shakes us to the marrow with its direct holy purity.

**Wine**

The experience of being filled with the Holy Spirit is compared to wine. The upper room group were mistaken for drunks when they had the initial experience of being baptized (or soaked in) and filled with the Holy Spirit.

> *Eph 5:18*
> *And do not get drunk with wine, for that is debauchery, but* ***be filled with the Spirit****,*

God put within us the desire for intoxication in His Spirit. He wants us to enjoy the euphoric, joyful pleasure of being drenched in His presence. Just as with all things, moderation is the key. If we stayed intoxicated in the new wine day and night we wouldn't be able to function in the earth and complete the mission God has for us. But every soldier needs liberty time for refreshing in the Spirit to fight battle fatigue.

> *Rom 14:17-18*
> *For the kingdom of God is not a matter of eating and drinking but of righteousness and peace and joy in the Holy Spirit. Whoever thus serves Christ is acceptable to God and approved by men.*

Wow. It says here that whoever serves God in righteousness, peace and joy is acceptable to God. These are the elementary invisible manifestations of the Kingdom made available to us by the Holy Spirit. So, drink up (in the Holy Spirit)! It's good for you.

*Prov 31:6-7*
*Give strong drink to the one who is perishing,*
*and wine to those in bitter distress;*
*let them drink and forget their poverty*
*and remember their misery no more.*

The wine, or strong drink, of the Spirit is given to anesthetize those who are "perishing," or about to die. In His mercy, many times the Lord will pour out the new wine just before He sends His fire to burn up the stuff He wants us rid of.

If we are to lay hold of our inheritance in Christ we must follow the narrow path He walked while on earth.[23] We must die to self and crucify all vestiges of things contrary to His character and will. If we are to partake of His glory, we must also partake of His sufferings.[24]

While we must embrace suffering and allow its work in our lives, it's not all about suffering. We should have eyes for balance in all things. Let suffering have its place and be thankful for its work in you. But take the wine of His Spirit when it's offered to you.

It's much less painful to go through the process of dying and spending some "quality time" on the cross if we are intoxicated with the Lord's love, peace, joy and beauty. So, at times an outpouring of wine may be an indication that His holy fire is coming.

## Fire

The Holy Spirit descended on the one hundred and twenty in the upper room like tongues of fire.[25] The fire of the Spirit comes to empower us. It gives us new boldness and understanding of the purposes of God for our lives. It energizes us to carry out the work of the Kingdom as flaming ministers of fire to be seen by the world.[26]

---

[23] 1 Jn 2:6
[24] 1 Pet 4:13, Rom 8:18-19, 2 Cor 1:4-5
[25] Acts 2:3
[26] Ps 104:4

Peter was made into a different man after the fire of God fell on him at Pentecost. Suddenly he had the revelation of the message of the Kingdom of God that Jesus had spoken of constantly while with him. Peter gave an exceptional sermon filled with revelation of the times and who Jesus was. He explained the meaning of the strange events happening that day with clarity and power.[27]

The fire of the Holy Spirit manifests in renewal meetings quite often. In fact, it shows up in our home regularly during prayer meetings as well. This type of fire has substance and produces heat that can significantly raise the temperature in a building. When touched by the fire many people will sweat and their skin will turn red and become very warm. The fire cleanses, empowers, and sparks new zeal for the Lord. It enables for service and brings the deposit of power needed for various types of ministry.

John the Baptist prophesied that Jesus would come to baptize, or completely immerse us in the Holy Spirit and fire.[28] Not only is this meant to empower and enable us to be His witnesses, fire is also used to purify and refine.[29] Many times, the fire of the Spirit comes to work a deeper process of refining within us. If we submit to this process, then the loss we might suffer when the fires of judgment come can be avoided. We need to be continually anointed and filled with the oil of the Holy Spirit so that fire has something to burn, besides us. The sweet oil of His presence provides fuel for the fire, so that we burn like a lamp wick without being consumed. Be one of the five wise virgins and soak in it and take plenty with you before you enter the fiery trials ahead.

Fire is also seen many times with, or on the periphery, of the cloud of glory. It comes just ahead of the smoky cloud to burn up all that is not pure and prepared to enter the holy realms of God's glory. This manifestation of fire seems to be a form of glory, rather than the energizing fire of the Holy Spirit. It is far more powerful and awesome.

---

[27] Acts 2:14-36
[28] Mt 3:11
[29] Mal 3:1-3

*Ex 24:17-18*
*Now the appearance of the glory of the* **LORD was like a devouring fire** *on the top of the mountain in the sight of the people of Israel. Moses entered the cloud and went up on the mountain.*

*Ex 19:18*
*Now Mount Sinai was wrapped in smoke because* **the LORD had descended on it in fire.**

*2 Chr 7:3*
*When all the people of Israel* **saw the fire come down and the glory of the LORD** *on the temple, they bowed down with their faces to the ground on the pavement and worshiped and gave thanks to the LORD, saying, "For he is good, for his steadfast love endures forever."*

*Ezek 1:4*
*As I looked, behold, a stormy wind came out of the north, and* **a great cloud, with brightness around it, and fire flashing forth continually**, *and in the midst of the fire, as it were gleaming metal.*

*Deut 5:22*
*"These words the LORD spoke to all your assembly at the mountain* **out of the midst of the fire, the cloud, and the thick darkness..."**

*Isa 10:16-17*
**and under his glory a burning will be kindled, like the burning of fire .**
*The light of Israel will become a fire,*
*and his Holy One a flame,*
*and it will burn and devour*
*his thorns and briers in one day.*

The fiery glory consumes all that cannot stand in the holy pure presence of the Lord. All things contrary to His will, and anything that does not find its origin and life in Him, will be reduced to ash by His great and terrible flame.

If we submit to the purifying fire of trials and tests, and continually seek to be filled with the oil of the Holy Spirit's anointing, we will be prepared for the fire of His glory. If we have been refined as gold then the fire of His glory will not bring judgment, but rather immense spiritual and natural blessing.

## Other Manifestations

Recorded accounts of revivals tell of odd physical manifestations in some people who were touched by the power of the Holy Spirit. Shaking, rolling on the ground, loss of physical strength and collapsing or falling down, various rapid motions of the limbs, head and torso, laughter and unusual words or sounds are commonly observed in people during powerful outpourings of the Holy Spirit. Many of these manifestations also seem to occur in conjunction with high levels of angelic activity.

These are all a physical response to heavenly power. When the power of God, or of angels, reaches certain levels of intensity the natural man (body and soul) will many times be affected and moved, or may be overcome altogether. Many report the sensation of electricity or heat during these times. Others report the feeling of wind. Some feel as if their body is being manipulated, like a puppet on strings. Though the motions may seem violent and beyond the natural ability of the human body at times, pain or injury are rarely, if ever, reported in connection with manifestations genuinely induced by the Spirit's power.

God respects the free will He has given each of us. He doesn't force Himself upon those who persistently resist Him. He will not bring fear or force those who are fearful of Him to do things against their will. Some manifestations can be controlled by a person experiencing them, if they will to stop them. However this usually diminishes, or altogether stops the flow of the Spirit. Manifestations are most likely to occur when we yield ourselves to the Holy Spirit and allow Him to take control.

Yet, I have experienced manifestations that were absolutely impossible to control to any great degree. On several occasions where there was powerful angelic activity I was unable to control the motions of my body and was overwhelmed by the power of angels. On one occasion in particular, by way of the gift of discerning of spirits, a number of people were made aware of a circular area roughly fifteen feet in diameter that was active with several powerful angels. Upon entering this "zone" of activity I had little control over the movement of my body. After "leaping" from the area of the angelic activity, I regained full control of myself. I took a second go at it, determined to maintain control of my body, and entered the area of activity again. As much as I tried, I found it impossible to keep from "dancing" and jerking about. Every person who dared to venture into this area was either sent sailing out of it, fell to the floor, or jerked around in indescribable ways

At times His presence, conviction and power can be so overwhelming that a physical response is mandatory. It has been common in outpourings of the past for people to fall to the ground, weep in sorrowful repentance under heavy conviction, and make unusual physical motions or sounds.

These types of manifestations are seen in those who have already been affected in their heart by the dealings of the Holy Spirit. In those who have hardened themselves, or rejected the promptings of God's Spirit, it seems that they usually have no awareness of His presence at all.

However, we must be careful not to judge someone who may not display outward signs of reaction or response to the presence of the Spirit. This is not necessarily due to a hardened heart, or any other issue of unrighteousness. At times God chooses to remove the sense of His presence from us to help in our spiritual development. Also, as we experience more of the power and presence of God our capacity to withstand levels of His presence increases. As we grow more accustomed to His manifest presence, we can stand without completely collapsing or displaying overt manifestations. Neither the existence, nor the absence, of manifestations is any indication of a person's spiritual condition or maturity.[30]

Some motions and vocal manifestations may have prophetic significance or may be symbolic. This is one way that the Holy

---

[30] 2 Cor 10:12

Spirit likes to make Himself known, and is a type of supernatural sign. For example, I remember being in a prayer meeting where people from a number of different nations were in attendance. As some were being prayed for they fell to the floor under the power of the Holy Spirit. One woman from France began to turn slowly in place as she, and her country, were prayed for. Several of us understood this to be a prophetic sign that France would be "turning" to the Lord.

I have also witnessed people roll over and back from side to side while lying on the floor under the power of God. On each occasion the tangible fire of the Holy Spirit was in manifestation. It was explained to me that the people were rolling to "put out the fire" that was on them. Though these people do not experience any pain, they do often feel heat, and the rolling motion seems to be involuntary. This particular manifestation is where the term "holy rollers" originated.

While manifestations are a sign that the Spirit is moving in power, we should not become focused on them or overly concerned about them. Many make the mistake of associating the manifestations with the presence of the Lord in an unhealthy way and will initiate manifestations themselves in an attempt to get the Spirit to move, or to appear "spiritual." The absence of manifestations does not necessarily mean that the Lord is not present in power.

Likewise, a person who is making unusual motions or sounds does not always indicate that the Holy Spirit is the source. Pastors and leaders must develop keen discernment to perceive the difference, and should always check it out with the Holy Spirit before taking action.

We should be careful not to incorrectly judge something unfamiliar to us as having its source in something other than God. Trying to stop someone from manifesting can grieve the Holy Spirit and could cause a visitation of God to end altogether. We should be careful to not be offended by what the Lord may choose to do through others, or try to control His manifest presence and power.

At the same time, the persistent and obvious disruptive behavior of someone trying to draw attention to their self should be addressed. Disorderly conduct is allowed to go on in some conference and renewal meetings these days, where a few people persistently scream, shout things out and cause general disruption while drawing attention to themselves at inappropriate times.[31] I understand the desire to err on the side of caution, and "taking the good with the bad" when God's Spirit moves.

    I hesitate to even include this paragraph, and urge all who read it to seek the Lord for proper discernment before acting on it. When individuals are obviously making commotion that is disruptive to the **true** flow of the Spirit within a gathering, it should be addressed. We should not let the immature behavior of a few interfere with the ability of others in attendance to partake of what God desires to impart. Paul addressed this issue with the carnal believers at Corinth in his first epistle to them.[32] In the same spirit of love and grace with which Paul wrote, great care should be taken to confront in love without trying to embarrass the person who may be "acting up," and help them to find a more appropriate avenue of expression.

    My reluctance to mention the above is because there are times when the Lord will cause an unusual manifestation that interrupts what is happening in the meeting at the moment, perhaps someone speaking, but is in the flow of what He desires to do. Again, keen spiritual discernment is needed before trying to stop things we don't understand or are not comfortable with at first. If in doubt, I think it best to err on the side of making room for the Spirit to move in the manner He sees fit at the time.

    For example, the Holy Spirit may cause someone (usually a woman, but not always) to have a "birthing" experience. The person will lie on the floor and make the same motions and sounds as a woman giving birth. This is a prophetic sign of the Lord's desire to bring to life something new in the Spirit for a region or group of people. Stopping the person who is birthing could abort the spiritual baby and grieve the Spirit. Sometimes letting the Lord have His way in our meetings can get messy and uncomfortable.

    Misjudging or misunderstanding the manifestations that may occur when the Spirit of God is at work in power can exact a price, as I found out several years ago. On the first night of a series of

---

[31] 1 Cor 14:40
[32] 1 Cor chapters 11-14

meetings I witnessed some unusual motions being made by a few people. I had not seen this particular type of manifestation before and wasn't sure if the Holy Spirit was the source. It just seemed pretty odd to me at first.

The next day I met my wife, Patti, at the airport as she was unable to make the first evening of the conference. On the drive to the meetings she asked how things went the night before and what I thought of the first session. I told her that the preaching was great and the presence of the Lord was definitely there. I must have had a grin on my face as she asked what was so funny. I chuckled a bit and said:

"You'll see."

"What do you mean? I'll see what?" she asked.

"Well, last night there were some folks manifesting in a way I haven't seen before. It was pretty wild. It will probably happen again tonight, so you'll see what I'm talking about," I answered.

"Manifestations like what? What were they doing?" she persisted.

"It's hard to describe. You might call it a 'fish dance" or something. They just make some pretty wild moves."

"Fish dance, huh?"

"Yeah, something like that," I said.

"So, is it God? What do you think?" she asked.

"Uh, I'm not sure. Could be. You'll see." I said

Well, sure enough the "fish dance" was in manifestation that night. Patti asked if what a few folks were doing was what I told her about.

"You mean this?" I said as I tried to imitate the movements being made by the people in question. "Yeah, that's the fish dance," I said laughing.

Just then I heard the voice of the Lord within me say "You think that's funny?"

"Uh-oh.," I thought. "Sorry Lord. I didn't mean to mock the work of your Spirit. It just seems a little weird. I didn't mean to offend you," I said silently.

"That's OK. But it's going to cost you," His voice boomed within me.

"Oh no. Cost me what, Lord?"

"Just your dignity," He said.

"Uh...what are you going to do, Lord?" I asked. ....Silence. "Oh no! Please. I'm sorry Lord... really!" ... More silence. "Great. I wonder what He's going to do to me," I thought.

Just then Patti said something like "Kevin! You shouldn't make fun of something that could be a work of the Spirit. Don't you think it could get you in trouble?"

"Uh, yeah. I think it could. That was stupid. I'm sorry" I said. I probably looked a little pale at that moment.

On the last night of the conference there was an altar call to receive prayer for specific things. Patti and I both went forward. She was blessed and fell under the power of the Spirit. When the person who prayed for her stepped over in front of me to pray, two other ministry team members came to assist. I think God let them in on His secret, because a couple of them were wearing mischievous grins.

Soon after they laid hands on me and began to pray I started to manifest in a way I never had before. I'm not sure what my body was doing, but I know just about every part of me that could move was in motion.

Patti got up off the floor at some point and started laughing at the spectacle I had become. I was so taken up by the amount of power I was experiencing that I wasn't really focused on what my body was doing. At first the laughter of the other people around me didn't catch my attention, as I figured they were just enjoying a little new wine of the Spirit. When I realized I was being laughed at, I tried to imagine what I looked like, but only for a moment – it was too painfully embarrassing. So, I just went with it – not that I had much of a choice really. I think I heard the Lord chuckle a little too.

Patti couldn't help but giggle about it the rest of the night, and the next day. Actually, she still does at times. "You do the 'fish dance' pretty well. Better than anyone else there." She would say while trying to contain her laughter.

I got off easy. God is so good, and He has a pretty good sense of humor too. A little justice and discipline while being drenched in His presence and receiving of His Spirit in power just speaks to me of His great mercy and love. Now I'm careful not to pass quick judgment about manifestations. I wait on the Holy Spirit to hear what He has to say about things that may seem odd at first. And I haven't done the "fish dance" since.

It is proper to carefully discern manifestations we may not be familiar or comfortable with at first by seeking the Lord for understanding. We should be careful not to be critical of or mock things we don't understand, as this could grieve the Spirit and possibly land us in trouble.

*1 Cor 1:27-29*
*But God chose what is foolish in the world to shame the wise; God chose what is weak in the world to shame the strong; God chose what is low and despised in the world, even things that are not, to bring to nothing things that are, so that no human being might boast in the presence of God.*

All of these manifestations are associated with the presence and working of the Holy Spirit, but they are not indicative of the manifest glory of God. As mentioned earlier in this chapter, much of the work of the Holy Spirit done through these various manifestations is designed to prepare us for the glory and to help us progress in our spiritual development.

While manifestations can be evidence of the Lord's work among us, their absence does not mean that He is not present or inactive. We should maintain proper perspective and keep our focus on the Lord, who is the source of these things, rather than on the manifestation or the people they may come through. We should seek the Lord and not His power or His various manifestations.

We should not view these things as the end of anything, but the means by which we might be made ready for greater things. In no way is this meant to diminish or minimize the importance and wonder of the Holy Spirit or His work in our lives. He is marvelous and amazing. His ministry (in part) is to lead us into all truth, transform us into the image of Christ, and glorify and make known the glory of Jesus and the Father.

A brief look at the ministry and gifts of the Holy Spirit and how He makes the way for us to enter heavenly realms will take us a step closer to understanding the glory.

## Activation

*Lord God, I thank You for the many manifestations of Your Spirit and for His work in my life. Please help me to understand and develop a healthy attitude toward the ways and workings of Your Spirit, as I grow in the knowledge of You. Amen.*

# Chapter 5
§

# In The Spirit

We considered some of the Holy Spirit's manifestations in chapter four, and saw that although He often moves in power, His manifest presence is not always in conjunction with the glory. In this chapter we will further contemplate the work and ministry of the Holy Spirit and see how He prepares and leads us into higher realms of spiritual experience.

Anointing is a word used to describe a number of things that are all ministrations of the Spirit of God. Today we refer to the divine power and authority bestowed upon a servant of the Lord as the anointing, as well. Many times the manifest tangible presence and power of God that is put upon ministers that is evident to others, is called the anointing.

An anointed musician is one who has a spiritual dynamic beyond the excellence of their natural musical talent. An anointed preacher would be one who effectively delivers a clear message with the power of the Holy Spirit, not just a polished orator. So, we may say that a person is anointed if they have a particular gift that is yielded to and empowered by the Holy Spirit to accomplish an effectual spiritual work.

Some servants of the Lord carry a strong anointing of His presence. Others have the ability to open up the realms of heaven and glory. While we should honor the chosen vessels of God and "touch not His anointed,"[33] we should also realize that the anointing a person carries is not necessarily an indication of the source or accuracy of the things they may say in prophecy or teaching.

---

[33] 1 Chr 16:22

Neither is it a sign of divine approval of their particular ministry style.

We are each individually responsible for carefully judging all teaching and prophecy before accepting it. I have seen many people led into error and deception by believing that the teaching or prophetic word of a minister was without error because of the strong anointing on the minister. This can get you into serious trouble and is a major cause for much of the false doctrine, and thus, the lack of power in the western church today.

There are many examples in history of men and women of God who walked in a powerful anointing who got off track by teaching or prophesying in error. Scripture documents several examples as well. Given to us as warnings, are tragic stories of God's anointed falling into sin, deception, and error, such as Saul, Baalam, David, and Solomon.

We must develop keen spiritual discernment. The days ahead will be wrought with peril for those who fail to discern error. Accuracy in prophecy is not indicative of the source of its inspiration. The slave girl in Acts 16:16-18 was "prophesying" with complete accuracy, but Paul discerned the source to be demonic. Getting to know the Source of the true anointing, and not just the anointing itself, will help you detect the false when it shows up.

The manifest presence of God can be experienced in certain places at certain times more readily than others. Often the Spirit of God will move apart from the physical presence of any particular person. This is also called the anointing, referring to the tangible presence of God that is present in a specific place.

Even though the Spirit of God may move so mightily that nearly all present are unable to stand in the power of His presence, this has rarely been due to a manifestation of the glory, in recent history. What many have mistakenly called the glory is in reality a strong outpouring of the anointing – the Holy Spirit.

The anointing oil used in the temple service of the Old Testament and for the ordination of kings and priests was used to confer the enabling power and authority to serve in a particular function, as commissioned by God. The oil itself is a type of the Holy Spirit. Mention of oil in Scripture many times is a reference to the Holy Spirit and receiving Him in fullness.

I realize that much of what follows may be "old hat" to you, but I think it is imperative to have a firm understanding of these things before proceeding. Some of you reading this book have experienced the baptism in the Holy Spirit and seek to be continually filled. Even so, I encourage you to read this section carefully. I believe it will help you communicate the truth, and the great importance of these things for every Christian, as you minister God's heart to others who have not yet received the Holy Spirit in fullness.

The Holy Spirit and all of His various gifts, endowments and manifestations are acquired by active faith. However, at the time of this book's writing, the predominate view in the church of North America concerning the Christian's filling with the Holy Spirit considers this to be a one time deposit made at conversion to Christ. Those who hold this view, see no need for a conscious decision to receive the Holy Spirit, nor any cooperative effort to acquire and maintain the ongoing filling of the Holy Spirit.

I personally find little scriptural support for these ideas. I also believe that this line of reasoning tends to form a mindset where the Holy Spirit becomes an impersonal force, rather than the third person of the Trinity. It fosters an unconscious denial of His personality. The Holy Spirit desires intimate personal relationship with us, just as the Father and the Son do.

He is a Gentleman and will not force Himself upon those who resist or ignore Him. He desires to be sought and accepted, not just taken for granted as a deposit placed within us by default, and then treated as a theoretical part of our spiritual lives. When we fail to recognize, desire, seek, obey, honor and come to know the Holy Spirit as Lord, Counselor, Comforter, Teacher and God, it grieves Him and limits His ministry in our lives. Both individually, and within the corporate Body of Christ. Failure in these things renders whatever Holy Spirit filling or baptism one claims less than theoretical. It is then, in fact, just an imagination of the convert.

I believe that everyone who comes to receive Christ has the Holy Spirit active in their lives to a certain degree. The knowledge of the truth of the gospel can come in no other way than by the work of the Holy Spirit. However, without the release and reception of the Holy Spirit by being totally immersed (baptized) in Him, I think that one can only have the Holy Spirit active in their life to the degree possible before Pentecost.

What Jesus has made available to us far surpasses the working of His Spirit in God's people before Pentecost. It is essential that we have the initial baptism experience to receive the Holy Spirit in fullness and then continually seek to be filled to overflowing with Him if we are to enter the reams of glory and enjoy all of the spiritual experiences that are part of our inheritance in Christ.

So that we might honor and come to know the Holy Spirit for the wonderful person and majestic God that He is, let's consider the role He should play in the life of every Christian and how we might come into experiential relationship with Him in reality.

The five wise virgins in the parable told by Jesus in Matthew chapter 25 not only kept their lamps filled with oil, but procured extra oil which they took with them in flasks. The oil here signifies the Holy Spirit. All ten in the story were virgins -- believers in Christ. But only the five wise virgins who carried the oil of the Holy Spirit were allowed into the wedding feast when the Bridegroom arrived.

Jesus considered this of great importance, as seen in the overall message of the parable and the consequences of not being a "wise virgin." Our Lord never spoke things that were not pertinent to His servants in all of the church age.[34] So, once understood, the parable must find application in the life of each believer today.

If baptism in the Holy Spirit, and the ongoing filling with Him, is independent of a volitional act of the individual Christian after conversion, then this parable would find no practical application and the admonition and warning it presents would be meaningless. If all believers are filled with and baptized in the Holy Spirit once, at initial conversion, then this parable lacks didactic (teaching) value, as there would be no possibility of being one of the foolish virgins.

Jesus spent a good amount of time teaching His disciples about the Holy Spirit in John chapters 14 through 16. His going to the Father in order that the Spirit could then be sent to them and dwell in them was emphasized in those chapters. If our Lord spent His

---

[34] Mk 13:37

last few hours with the twelve teaching about this, how much more should we consider this of paramount concern to us?

Just before His betrayal, trial, torture and death the Lord comforts His closest friends with the promise of the Holy Spirit. He assures them that He will be with them always by His Spirit. To refuse such aid, or any part of what Christ paid for in His unimaginable sufferings, is nothing less than an insult to Him. It is to treat the cross and His sacrifice with contempt.

John the Baptist prepared the way and pointed to the one who would come and baptize in the Holy Spirit and fire.[35] The culmination of Christ's redemptive work after His ascension was to send the Holy Spirit to all who would believe.[36] He placed the greatest importance on this, and so should we.

Yet this is the most common form of disobedience in the church today. We grieve Him by neglecting, or refusing altogether, the baptism and ongoing filling of the Holy Spirit. All acts of service, worship, and sacrifice are made acceptable to God only if they are motivated and empowered by the Holy Spirit. We quench the Spirit of God if we fail to respond to His promptings, prophecies, direction, and conviction. His work is resisted by trying to squelch His gifts, manifestations or those He desires to move through.[37]

The baptism of the Holy Spirit is considered an optional "gift" by many in the church today. However, this is not how Scripture portrays speaking in tongues and the ministry of the Holy Spirit. Jesus commanded His disciples to receive the Holy Spirit. He did not make it optional.

*John 20:21-22*
*Jesus said to them again, "Peace be with you. As the Father has sent me, even so I am sending you." And when he had said this, he breathed on them and said to them,* ***"Receive the Holy Spirit."***

The Lord commanded them to receive. So, there was a conscious decision to cooperate needed on the disciples' part to

---

[35] Mt 3:11
[36] Jn 14:12-22
[37] 1 Thes 5:19-22

receive the impartation of the Holy Spirit, who would be made available to them in just a few days.

However, Jesus' act of blowing and instructing them to receive was not the baptism, or impartation, of the Holy Spirit. It was a prophetically symbolic act of the wind of the Spirit that would blow upon them at Pentecost. Jesus would not have instructed them to receive the Holy Spirit if this had already been accomplished through the act of His blowing on them.

Therefore it required a volitional decision and cooperative effort on the part of the disciples. The reception of the indwelling Holy Spirit and baptism in the Holy Spirit are not two different events, but one and the same. The Holy Spirit is not given at conversion, but at "Pentecost."

The twelve had already believed in and received Jesus as Messiah, Savior and Lord. Yet the Lord instructed them to receive the Holy Spirit. This was a command that they would not come to fulfill nor understand until a short time later.

This is similar in nature to the "Great Commission" Jesus gave in Mark 16:15. Though He gave a command to the disciples they were not expected to commence the work ordered immediately. They were to wait for the power and enablement to be His witnesses and carry out the commission. So it is with the Lord's instruction to receive the Spirit in John 20:22. Actually, the obedience to one command (to wait for the power of the Spirit) made obedience to the other possible.

Accounts in the book of Acts further prove the baptism in the Holy Spirit is a separate event from repentance and coming to accept Jesus as Lord. After spending forty days teaching His disciples about the Kingdom of God prior to His ascension, Jesus told them to go into Jerusalem and wait for the Holy Spirit to come upon them and give them power to become His witnesses.[38] Even after spending more than three years with Jesus, seeing all of the miraculous signs He performed, witnessing His death, burial, and resurrection, His closest disciples failed to grasp the meaning of the Lord's teaching about the Kingdom of God. They were still looking for Him to establish a political Kingdom on earth at that time.

---

[38] Acts 1:3-8

As was the Lord's way many times when asked questions, He seemed to avoid giving an answer to the question of whether He would restore the kingdom to Israel. But in actuality He gave a more complete answer than the hearers understood, until later. On one hand His answer seemed to say "No, not at this time." Then He said that they would receive power when the Holy Spirit came upon them. So, in another sense He was telling them that the Kingdom of God would be established in them not many days hence, when the Holy Spirit would be given them. We see in Acts chapter 2 that the event the Lord had prophesied came to pass on the day of Pentecost. Along with the supernatural signs of a mighty rushing wind and of fire appearing on the heads of those in the upper room, they began to speak in other tongues.

Though Jesus commissioned them to go into the entire world to preach the gospel and do His works, they were told to wait until the Holy Spirit came upon them to empower them for service as His witnesses. This is still applicable to each of us today. There is an abundance of non-Spirit filled or non-empowered work being done in His name. We should first wait to be enabled by the Holy Spirit for the specific work He calls us to before entering into it. Not only in receiving the initial baptism in Holy Spirit, but also before embarking on any new work He may commission. That is, we must seek to be continually filled with His Spirit.

Only days before the Pentecost events, these men were rather confused about the true meaning of the Lord's teaching on the Kingdom of Heaven. Suddenly, they were radically transformed in their thinking as the Holy Spirit revealed to them deeper spiritual truth about all that they heard and saw while Jesus walked on earth with them. Peter, who (though zealous for the Lord) had been seriously deficient in his comprehension of the gospel, stands before a crowd of thousands and articulates a sermon so filled with life and supernatural revelation by the Spirit, that thousands come to know Christ after hearing it. They were all changed into different people by the power that came upon them.

The word *baptism* is a transliteration of the Greek word used in the New Testament to describe several different things that every Christian should be immersed in. It means to be completely submersed into something; to be soaked and fully saturated in a substance. The words *baptism* and *receive* are synonymous as used in reference to the Holy Spirit in the New Testament. To receive the Holy Spirit is the same in meaning as being baptized in Him. Eternal life, living water, and the Kingdom of Heaven are all expressions that refer to the transforming work, ministry, and immersion in the Holy Spirit. Without the conscious seeking for and reception of the Holy Spirit the work of regeneration is incomplete in the individual believer.

This is what John the Baptist, and Jesus talked so much about in the Gospels[39] -- the all encompassing, saturating life of the Spirit that would be made available to all who would believe and receive. To lack the complete immersion in the Spirit of God is to lack eternal life. To refuse Him and His work in us is to refuse the only means by which we can be "saved" -- to be transformed by the power of the Holy Spirit in the process of salvation.

Normal initiation into the Body of Christ requires four basic things to be done by the new believer:

- Repent of dead works (e.g sin, self righteousness, self effort, legalism, or religion as a means of gaining righteousness)
- Put total faith in God and the completed redemptive work of Christ Jesus
- Be baptized in water
- Be baptized in (receive) the Holy Spirit

These are all part of the elementary doctrine of Christ.[40] If the foundation isn't laid properly or completed, then there is no hope for building a sound structure. If we lack the correct understanding, or have not obeyed in completing the basic steps of initiation into Christ, we cannot progress toward maturity and obtain the promise of every spiritual blessing that God desires to give us.[41]

In every instance recorded in the book of Acts where the baptism of the Holy Spirit is documented, the one being baptized

---

[39] Mt 3:11
[40] Heb 6:1-3
[41] Eph 1:3

spoke in other tongues. This is the normative experience when one is baptized in the Spirit. It should be the experience of all believers.

*Acts 10:44-47*
*While Peter was still saying these things, the **Holy Spirit fell on** all who heard the word. And the believers from among the circumcised who had come with Peter were amazed, because the **gift of the Holy Spirit was poured out** even on the Gentiles. For they were hearing them **speaking in tongues** and extolling God. Then Peter declared, "Can anyone withhold water for baptizing these people, who have **received the Holy Spirit** just as we have?"*

Peter recognized speaking in tongues as being the evidence that the people in this passage had received the Holy Spirit. Notice that it says that the *"Holy Spirit fell on"* those listening. This is similar to the initial outpouring on those in the upper room on Pentecost. It is the same in outward manifestation and purpose as the initial Pentecost outpouring.

Jesus said that speaking in different tongues would be one of the signs that accompanies believers.[42] Paul admonished those he taught to receive the baptism in the Holy Spirit and encouraged all believers to speak in tongues.[43]

Baptism in the Holy Spirit, as evidenced by speaking in tongues, was considered normative and compulsory for all Christians in the early church, as we can see from the above verses and those to follow shortly. Those who had not received the Holy Spirit as evidenced by speaking in tongues, were taught the Way more accurately and brought into the fullness of their spiritual birth by those who understood the imperative need for such.

*Acts 18:24-26*
*Now a Jew named Apollos, a native of Alexandria, came to Ephesus. He was an eloquent man, competent in the Scriptures. He had been instructed in the way of the Lord.*

---

[42] Mk 16:17-18
[43] 1 Cor 14:4-5, 1 Cor 14:18

*And being fervent in spirit, he spoke and taught accurately the things concerning Jesus, **though he knew only the baptism of John**. He began to speak boldly in the synagogue, but when Priscilla and Aquila heard him, **they took him and explained to him the way of God more accurately**.*

Apollos only knew the baptism of John, which is in water, signifying repentance. Even though Apollos was well educated in the other aspects of the gospel message, he had not completely understood what was needed to receive the fullness of Jesus. Much of the church today is in the same state of ignorance of these truths.

While Apollos was ignorant, he was also teachable and received the instruction of Priscilla and Aquila. Oh, that this could be said of all who lack the reality of the Spirit in their lives today! It is grievous that so many have taken a hostile stance against the great Gift not only offered to, but commanded to be received by, all who come to Christ in full faith and true repentance.

*Acts 19:1-7*
*And it happened that while Apollos was at Corinth, Paul passed through the inland country and came to Ephesus. There he found some disciples. And he said to them, **"Did you receive the Holy Spirit when you believed?"** And they said, "No, we have not even heard that there is a Holy Spirit." And he said, "Into what then were you baptized?" They said, **"Into John's baptism."** And Paul said, "John baptized with the baptism of repentance, telling the people to believe in the one who was to come after him, that is, Jesus." On hearing this, they were baptized in the name of the Lord Jesus. And when Paul had laid his hands on them, **the Holy Spirit came on them, and they began speaking in tongues** and prophesying. There were about twelve men in all.*

Again we see that receiving the Holy Spirit is separate and subsequent to initial belief, or faith in Christ. If the Holy Spirit is automatically installed within the new convert at the time they acknowledge Christ's Lordship and put their trust in Him for salvation, then the question Paul asked those at Ephesus in Acts 19:2 would make no sense. Paul would not have asked them if they had received the Holy Spirit when they first believed if the Holy Spirit takes up residence in the new believer automatically.

These were, no doubt, the disciples of Apollos who would have lacked the fullness of the gospel message, just as he had. When Paul found that their initiation into Christ was incomplete, he immediately took steps to remedy this. Just as Priscilla and Aquila recognized the crucial need for what was lacking in Apollos and addressed it with him, so also Paul understood the perilous condition of those taught by Apollos and corrected the situation.

Yet for the sake of "unity" and "love," (for political correctness and for fear of man really) most of the Charismatic/Pentecostal wing of the church today shrinks away from speaking the truth in love to our brethren who have not yet received the Holy Spirit. If we truly understood the great importance of these things, we would see that in reality our silence is un-loving and serving to further divide us.

Just as Paul, Priscilla and Aquila presented the truth more accurately to the believers who lacked the fullness of their spiritual birth, so should we teach and admonish, with gentle humility, those who lack the same today. True unity will not come about by avoiding matters of controversy, but by speaking the truth in love. We are only one if we are one in The Spirit.

A single chapter won't afford a complete presentation of these topics. So, I strongly recommend that you study and consider these things for yourself in greater depth. I highly recommend two books by David Pawson; *"The Normal Christian Birth"*[44] and *"Jesus Baptizes in One Holy Spirit"*.[45] These are both excellent resources that cover the assertions I have made here with depth and clarity.

We must also seek to be continually filled with the Spirit, moment by moment. The initial deposit is not enough to carry you through the rest of your life. We tend to leak the anointing. We have continual need to place ourselves before Him to receive increasing measures of His Spirit.

---

[44] *Hoder & Soughton UK 1989*
[45] *Hoder & Soughton UK 1997*

The five wise virgins in the parable took along extra oil.[46] This speaks of our need to wait upon the Lord and be filled to overflowing with His Spirit – the anointing oil of the Lord. Being "Spirit filled" does not mean that we have received the baptism in the Holy Spirit and speak in tongues, but that we are habitually being filled with His righteousness, peace and joy. It is to learn to operate out of the store of spiritual oil within us. This brings our thoughts, words and actions into agreement with the indwelling Spirit of God. To think, do or say anything contrary to the nature and will of the Holy Spirit within us grieves Him, causing us to leak the oil and lose our position of victory over the flesh, sin and the world.

Persistent quenching of the Spirit sears the conscience and eventually leads one into the most dangerous state of deception. Without the God given grace for repentance, the end is the complete loss of sensitivity to the Holy Spirit, with no hope of recovery. The loss of the Person and power that is given to complete the work of salvation within us leaves no possibility of recovering eternal life for those who ignore and neglect Him to the point of complete insensitivity. There are very clear warnings in Scripture concerning this.[47]

Our spiritual inheritance can only be accessed if we are "in the Spirit." So, we must have completed our initiation into His Body, and then seek to be continually filled, through obedience, seeking, and waiting on the Holy Spirit in faith.

In no way am I suggesting that the free gifts of eternal life and everything made available to those who trust in Jesus are withheld until we become holy enough. Neither do I suggest they can be earned. Yet, we must respond to Him and seek the Spirit filled life to be made ready to receive all that He has for us.[48]

Some are reluctant to speak in tongues or to pursue the things of the Spirit for fear of being deceived, or being influenced by demons. The Lord promised us that if we ask Him for the Holy Spirit He will not give us something evil.[49] The devil has no legal right to give us

---

[46] Mt 25:1-13
[47] Beb 2:1-3, Heb 6:4-8, Eph 4:30-31
[48] Mt 7:7-11
[49] Lk 11:9-13

anything if we are asking God for His Spirit. The Lord won't allow us to receive anything false, if we have come to true repentance and faith in Christ, and ask for His Spirit.

The supernatural may seem frightening to those unfamiliar with it, and many people don't like the thought of "losing control." But that is the purpose of receiving and being filled with the Spirit – to become emptied of self and to yield to the Holy Spirit in progressively greater ways. In reality, seeking spiritual things apart from the protective guidance of the Holy Spirit presents the greater danger.

The gifts of the Spirit cannot be obtained apart from receiving the baptism in the Holy Spirit and their use should not be pursued apart from the ongoing filling of the Spirit. I personally am not aware of anyone who operates in true prophetic, healing, or other gifts of the Spirit who does not speak in tongues. If we put forth the idea that the gifts are available apart from the baptism and filling of the Holy Spirit it is likely to lead those who lack the Spirit filled life to fall into serious deception, and possibly come under demonic influence.

The Holy Spirit is given to lead us into all truth[50], and apart from His filling and leading we make ourselves vulnerable to counterfeit "gifts," experiences, and influences. Seeking the gifts of the Spirit or, any other spiritual experience, apart from the continual filling and maintenance of a pure heart can be dangerous. If you have not been baptized in the Holy Spirit, or if you are not living a life of progressive growth in holiness and obedience to Him, I would caution against operating in any of the spiritual gifts or seeking after spiritual experience until you get things right with the Lord.

It is also important to understand that operating in the supernatural gifts of the Holy Spirit,[51] is no indication of ones spiritual maturity. The believers at Corinth were zealous for the things of the Holy Spirit and His gifts, but it is plain that they were seriously deficient in the outworking of love. Paul encouraged them to become proficient in their understanding and use of the gifts of the Holy Spirit, while maturing and pursuing love above all else.

---

[50] Jn 16:13
[51] 1 Cor 12:7-11

Growing in the knowledge of God, and in His love, are what lead to maturity, while spiritual gifts are given as tools for our edification, and to enable us to do the Lord's work in the earth.[52] Thus we see Paul place 1 Corinthians 13's teaching on love in the middle of His writings concerning spiritual gifts.

Because some have pursued the gifts of the Holy Spirit and have neglected the development of their character, others have mistakenly associated the use of His gifts with carnality. The gifts are available to all believers regardless of the level of their development in character and love. To then think that one must be forsaken for the other is also a serious mistake.

Paul insists that we not be found lacking in either spiritual gifts, or in maturity.[53] We are admonished to earnestly desire the gifts, while pursing love above all.[54] The use of our individual spiritual gifts should be motivated and empowered by love. The gifts are nothing, if God's heart is not communicated in their use. The good news is that we can, and should, have both in full measure.

*Eph 1:3*
*Praise be to the God and Father of our Lord Jesus Christ, who has blessed us in the **heavenly realms** with every spiritual blessing in Christ.*
*NIV*

The operative phrase in Eph 3:1 that indicates the condition for obtaining these blessings in reality, and not just in theory, is ***"in Christ."*** So, what are the conditions to being found *"in Christ"* and how can we know that we are truly in Him?

*John 3:36*
*Whoever believes in the Son has eternal life; whoever **does not obey** the Son shall not see life, but the wrath of God remains on him.*

---

[52] 1 Cor 12:7
[53] 1 Cor 1:7, Eph 4:13, Col 1:28
[54] 1 Cor 14:1

Jesus also taught us to abide in Him.[55] The measure of our abiding in Jesus, and He in us, is the measure of His love that we show for one another.

*2 Cor 13:5*
*Examine yourselves, to see whether you are in the faith. Test yourselves. Or do you not realize this about yourselves, that **Jesus Christ is in you**? — unless indeed you fail to meet the test!*

So, what is the test or indication that Christ is in us and that we are in Him and in the faith?

**Obedience**

*Col 2:6-7*
*Therefore, as you received Christ Jesus the Lord, **so walk in him**, rooted and built up in him and **established in the faith**, just as you were taught, abounding in thanksgiving.*

*1 John 2:3-6*
*And by this we know that we have come to **know him**, if we **keep his commandments**. Whoever says "I know him" but does not keep his commandments is a liar, and the truth is not in him, but whoever keeps his word, in him truly the love of God is perfected. **By this we may be sure that we are in him**: whoever says he abides in him ought to **walk in the same way in which he walked**.*

We can be sure that we are in the faith and growing into His likeness if we consistently walk in obedience to His commands, both written and revealed. The Holy Spirit was sent to enable us to both hear and fulfill the active prophetic Word of the Lord. To refuse the ministry of the Holy Spirit is to refuse the means by which we are able to know and obey the specific will of God for our lives. It is to refuse intimate communion with God. It is impossible to "know

---

[55] Jn 15:11-17

Him" if we do not obey Him. This can be by way of direct disobedience or by neglecting to seek Him to hear His voice and understand His unique will for us individually.

We are *"in Him"* if we walk as Jesus Himself walked while on earth. Christ is our example and our standard. Jesus did only what He saw His Father doing and said only what the Father said.[56] This is the pinnacle of obedience.

Though most of us have not yet apprehended this level of absolute obedience, it is the standard which we must mature towards nevertheless. Paul understood this as the measure of his own progress toward obtaining the fullness of his inheritance in Christ.[57]

> *Phil 3:10-16*
> *that I may know him and the power of his resurrection, and **may share his sufferings**, becoming like him in his death, that by any means possible I may attain the resurrection from the dead. **Not that I have already obtained this or am already perfect, but I press on to make it my own**, because Christ Jesus has made me his own. Brothers, I do not consider that I have made it my own. But one thing I do: forgetting what lies behind and straining forward to what lies ahead, I press on toward the goal for the prize of the upward call of God in Christ Jesus. Let those of us who are mature think this way, and if in anything you think otherwise, God will reveal that also to you. Only let us hold true to what we have attained.*

## Holiness

God commands us to be holy even as He is holy.[58] Yet Paul describes his own struggles with his humanity and the personal battle to do the things God desires rather than the things his sinful nature desired.[59] If Paul had difficulty fulfilling the spiritual requirements of God's law, what victory can we expect?

---

[56] Jn 5:19-20
[57] See also Heb 5:8-10, 2 Cor 10:4-6
[58] Lev 1:44-45, 1 Pet 1:16
[59] Rom 7:15-25

By setting our minds, or meditating, on the things of the Spirit we facilitate the ongoing filling of the Holy Spirit within us.[60] The continual filling with the Holy Spirit is the fuel of transformation and the oil that produces the spiritual illumination needed for us to comprehend and apply truth. Thus we grow into fulfilling the holy standard of taking on the likeness of Christ.

**Love one another**

By this we know that we are in Him and that He is in us: that we love the Lord God in the truest and fullest sense, and that we love one another with the love He has given us. We fulfill His requirement of holiness as we walk habitually and with increasing consistency in His Spirit. We have come to know Him and abide in Him if we love one another with the same love with which He loves us – the love of the Father.

In His mercy and great love for us He blesses us, even when we are not in the spiritual condition we should be. Without His gracious offer to give us all things that pertain to life and godliness[61] we would be without hope altogether. He is patient and long suffering, and totally committed to transforming us into His image.

Yet, many have taken a casual attitude toward their part in the sanctifying work of the Spirit in their lives. While we cannot bring about the changes that God requires by ourselves apart from the Holy Spirit, we must exert effort in our cooperation with His work in our lives for transformation to take place.

So, with a proper foundation laid, we're ready to move on to the heavenly places prepared for those who are in the Spirit of Christ.

---

[60] Rom 8:4-11
[61] 2 Pet 1:3

**Activation**

I encourage you to seek for a greater filling of the Holy Spirit in you and to seek to be continually filled. This is one prayer that is certain to be answered by God.[62]

*Father God, I ask that You would fill me to overflowing with Your Holy Spirit. Lord, teach me to live a life that is pleasing to You and attractive to the Holy Spirit. Help me to hear the voice of Your Spirit within me with clarity and help me to obey all that You command. I thank You for the enabling work and gifts that You have made available to me by way of Your Spirit. Thank You for the sanctifying work of transformation that You desire to work in me, Holy Spirit. Help me to yield and cooperate with the things You desire to do in me and through me. I choose to actively seek for more of Your presence and for deeper intimacy with the Spirit of Jesus and to lay hold of all that Christ has purchased for me. All blessing be yours forever, Lord. Amen.*

---

[62] Mt 7:11, Mt 7:7, Lk 11:13, Lk 12:32

# Chapter 6
## §

# Heavenly Places

"I'm traveling rapidly through clouds and mistsss...SHHH....SSHHHH....and now I see...uh ...its getting black and I see ssstars...WHOOOOA!" Her voice shuddered and her breathing was convulsive as her body shook while she described this trip into the heavens, as it happened. The presence of the Lord was thick and weighty in the room where about two hundred people had gathered to learn more about heavenly realms.

"I've stopped traveling now," her speech became more relaxed and her breathing began to slow. Her body quivered only slightly.
"Um... I see um... I'm in a beautiful green field and I see a large white HOOORSSSE.... HOOOOO!"

There she goes again with the shaking and all. And now I'm seeing exactly what she's describing just before she speaks it out. I looked around the room and could tell that nearly thirty or forty percent of the others there were having the same experience as well.

The horse I saw in this vision was very large and muscular. It was pure white, except for its mane, which was golden. Its eyes were fiery and flames came from its nostrils as it exhaled in furious blasts. Its countenance was fierce and focused. This creature was on a mission. It charged one way and then another as it flung its head about leaving trails of golden flakes and fire.

"And uh...the horse is running across the field and um....wherever the horse steps it leaves FFFIIIRE behind in the footprints...SHHH.....SHHHHHH!" she went on.

I could barely stand under the intense power being released in the room as I watched the vision along with many others. It was terrifying and beautiful. The sight of this creature would strike fear in the heart of the most battle hardened warrior.

I was amazed by the sights and by the knowledge that so many of us were all experiencing the same thing. We had entered into a heavenly realm together and were witnessing all of this in real time. I verified this with a number of folks later on, who all reported seeing and hearing what was described by the woman who was "launched" into the third heaven. We were all amazed when we compared the details of this vision, as we had perceived them.

During the experience I asked the Lord about the horse and what it was doing. He told me that it was the horse He will ride when He returns to Earth and that it is ready to go and increasingly restless as the time draws near. Whoa!

Open visions of angels, chariot rides with angels, and the manifest fire of God were among the many spiritual treats we enjoyed during this week of heavenly realm exploration. This is the stuff we've been made for. It's part of your inheritance. Don't let it go wasted!

We regularly have visionary experiences and the fire of God manifest, in our meetings. One of our favorite things to do is to launch people into the heavenly realms to be led into places of wonder by angels, or the Lord of Glory Himself. We try to make room for the Holy Spirit to do as He pleases. Sometimes it's just hanging out and having a meal with our friends and sharing what the Lord is doing in our lives. Other times there's some teaching or praying or prophecy or just soaking in His presence. We love to explore the heavenly realms and operate in our gifts to bless one another and share times of encouragement and refreshing in the Lord.

But the glory is something beyond these things. At times we get glimpses of the glory realm, but we are hungry to have it come in greater fullness. The line of definition between the glory and other heavenly experiences is not clearly defined. I think that we move from realms of anointing and the weighty presence of God into realms of glory in stages, but they are without absolute boundaries.

Manifestations, or tokens, of the glory are sometimes given to us as well. On occasion we have seen the golden flakes of glory appear. I think this is a sign that we are on the outskirts of the glory. It makes us want to pursue Him more until we have the fullness of the glory among us.

So, just how many "heavens" are there, anyway? Some suggest that there are only three heavens clearly defined in Scripture, citing the reference to the "third heaven" used by Paul in describing an experience he had.[63] But are there only three "heavens"? Let's see if we can find the answer by examining more than one passage.

*John 14:2-3*
*In my Father's house are many rooms. If it were not so, would I have told you that I go to prepare a place for you? And if I go and prepare a place for you, I will come again and will take you to myself, that where I am you may be also.*

The many rooms, or mansions, that Jesus spoke of here are the many dimensions and realms of heaven. These are our inheritance, not heavenly houses prepared for us to inhabit when we die. They are places prepared for us by our loving Father that are waiting to be discovered and thoroughly explored with Him. It has always been His plan for us to begin our exploration of these many rooms with Him now, in this life. The adventure will continue and progress throughout eternity as our union with Him becomes more complete.

Paul also spoke of multiple heavenly places or realms in Eph 1:3, 20, 2:6, 3:10, 6:12.

In Revelation 1:10 John says that he was *"in the Spirit on the Lord's Day."* There are various interpretations that have been popularly taught on the meaning of the phrase *"on the Lord's day."* One is that it refers to the first day of the week. Early Christians gathered to worship the Lord on Sunday. So, some see this as indicating the particular day of the week on which John received the

---

[63] 2 Cor 12:2

Revelation of Jesus Christ. Another suggests that it refers to "The Day of the Lord" in the eschatological (study of last things, or the last days) sense. This view would have John transported into the future in the Spirit to witness events of the great and terrible Day of the Lord.

The phrase *"in the Spirit"* used by John here, should not be taken in the same way in which Paul frequently used the phrase. Paul used this term to indicate the perpetual spiritual, emotional, mental, and physical states of being of one who is yielded to and filled with the Holy Spirit, as a normal part of the Christian life. John, however, is indicating an unusual state of heavenly or ecstatic spiritual experience, as evidenced by the fuller context of the passage, and by his use of the same phrase elsewhere in the book of Revelation.[64]

John is already having an extreme experience with the Lord at this point in Revelation chapter one. We see that he was in the Spirit, both in the sense of an ongoing disciplined Christian life, and in reference to the spiritual vision he is describing. Yet, a little later in Revelation chapter 4 John's experience takes a turn as he is called by God into a higher realm.

> *Rev 4:1-2*
> *After this I looked, and behold, a door standing open in heaven! And the first voice, which I had heard speaking to me like a trumpet, said, "Come up here, and I will show you what must take place after this."* ***At once I was in the Spirit***, *and behold, a throne stood in heaven, with one seated on the throne.*

Without a doubt, John was *"in the Spirit"* in every sense of the phrase prior to being called up through the open door he saw in "heaven." If John describes the door he saw as being in heaven, then where was he when he saw it? And where was he earlier in chapters 1, 2 and 3? Then he says that *"at once I was in the Spirit."* Wasn't he already in the Spirit?

---

[64] Rev 4:2, 17:3, 21:10

Later in the Revelation John is again taken in the Spirit to yet another dimension, or realm of heaven.

> *Rev 21:9-11*
> *"Come, I will show you the Bride, the wife of the Lamb." And **he carried me away in the Spirit** to a great, high mountain, and showed me the holy city Jerusalem coming down out of heaven from God, **having the glory of God**, its radiance like a most rare jewel, like a jasper, clear as crystal.*

Throughout the various visionary experiences he chronicles, John was taken from one dimension of heaven to another and from one state of being *"in the Spirit'* to higher realms. All of this would seem to support the existence of more than three heavens. At least it would show there are multiple dimensions or realms within the "third heaven."

## Seated with Christ

Access to these realms is granted to all those who are in Christ.

> *Eph 1:3*
> *Praise be to the God and Father of our Lord Jesus Christ, who has blessed us in the **heavenly realms** with every spiritual blessing in Christ.*
> NIV

Paul says here that we are blessed with *every* spiritual blessing in the ***heavenly realms*** in Christ. Again, Paul refers to heavenly places, or realms, in the plural. So, if you are ***in Christ*** every spiritual blessing and experiences in the heavenly realms are freely given to you. The heavenly realms and every spiritual blessing are yours to be accessed by faith.

Some teach that the spirit of the Christian is ever before the throne of God. This well known passage in Ephesians is used as the support for this supposition:

*Eph 2:4-6*
*But God, being rich in mercy, because of the great love with which he loved us, even when we **were** dead in our trespasses, made us alive together with Christ — by grace you have been saved — and raised us up with him and seated **us with him in the heavenly places in Christ Jesus**,*

One theological position concerning our access to the throne of God and the realms of heaven states that our spirits are continually stationed there without regard for our awareness of being there. This line of thinking usually gives little consideration to the spiritual condition of the individual or the reality of such positioning being made known in actual experience. I call this theoretical or positional theology. It states what is potentially ours and what is made available to each Christian.

But the acquisition of the promises of God, in reality and experience, is always conditional. We have seen that the condition to making the possession and enjoyment of *every spiritual blessing in the heavenly places* manifest in our experience in this natural life is abiding *"in Christ."* Just as positional theology would place all who claim the name of Jesus to be seated with Him in heavenly places, this view would also have every confessing Christian *"in Christ,"* without regard for the conditional aspects of being in Him in reality.

I think true Christians are seated with Christ in theory, but many are not seated with Him in reality. Paul is explaining that the position we have in Christ is not based on our own efforts or works, but is the gift of God given even when we **were** (past tense, indicating repentance has taken place) living in unrepentant sin. This applies to the believer who has made the sanctifying work of the Holy Spirit effectual and constant in their life. Nothing in this passage negates the condition of obedience for the process of salvation to be a reality. We are seated with Christ and have access to His throne to the degree that we have allowed Him to establish His throne of rule in our lives and have made a place for Him to rest His head.

## The Throne Room

The author of Hebrews[65] gives us instruction to *"draw near to the throne of grace"*.[66] This is an act of our own volition as we recognize the grace made available to us, by Christ, to overcome temptation and progress in the work of sanctification. This is further evidence that we are not positioned before the throne of God by default, but must approach it in humility, reverence and confidence in the Lord's great love and mercy for us.

Approaching *"the throne of grace"* is likely an expression used to describe our position in prayer before God as we are in Christ, rather than a reference to visionary visits to the Throne Room. So, true "Throne Room" experiences are probably less frequent than what has been reported by some.

However, Throne Room encounters will become far more common as we approach the culmination of His reconciling all things unto Himself in these last days. I am not calling into question the experiences of any particular person or their claims to have visited the Throne Room. But I believe that our experiences will become more vivid and defined as we progress in the things of the Spirit corporately and individually.

To date, I have had just a few "Throne Room" encounters. During one[67] visit, I was so awestruck by the glorious light radiating from the Lord that the compunction to worship overwhelmed me. I fell face down on the sea of glass like crystal.[68] I was curious about this enormous plane of spiritual substance, and my spirit whispered questions to the Lord about it.

> "Holy! Lord, you are amazing. What is this vast sea that I am lying on made of?" I asked.

> "What is the foundation of My Throne?" came the question back.

---

[65] Paul is in all likelihood the author of the Book of Hebrews
[66] Heb 4:15-16
[67] To be accurate, this experience actually occurred over two visits to the Throne Room, but is written as if it happened on one. More on this shortly
[68] Rev. 4

"Righteousness and justice, Lord?"

"And in what manner must you worship Me?" He asked

"In Spirit and Truth, Lord."

"Yes, very good. What you are supported by here is righteousness and truth -- the very emanation of my Throne. It is pure and incorruptible. My sovereign reign over all that is, or ever will be, is supported by My righteousness and truth. Remember that while in my mortal body I said that I Am Truth. It is the substance of what the elders, and angels, and living creatures and all who come here stand on in their worship to Me. It is without end. You are able to stand on it as you embrace truth and receive righteousness in My Son, who has justified you because of My great mercy. The sea of glass also represents My steadfast mercy. My justice is supported by my infinite mercy, making My judgments righteous," He explained gently.

"Thank you, Father. You are so good to me! It is clear like glass or crystal. What can I see through it, Lord?" I asked.

"It is not what you can see *through* it, but what you can see *in* it that matters" He said.

"I don't understand, Lord. Please explain."

"Put your face into the sea of glass" He said.

What was solid gave way as I pushed my face into it. It molded itself around my head as I pressed deeper in. I began to see and hear things in the substance. It was like a panoramic view of different visions, or doorways into other dimensions. I was able to choose from a myriad of visions displayed around me. As I focused upon one it would take on more detail.

I don't recall many details about the various visions and gateways I saw. The experience ended abruptly soon after I put my face into the sea of glass like crystal. This has happened during other heavenly voyages, where I am briefly introduced to something new, and then the experience ends suddenly. Sometimes I am taken back to further explore or understand what I got a glimpse of earlier. I think this was an initiatory experience and I am hoping that I will be given the opportunity to further explore the wonders that are in the sea of glass.

As I mentioned a little earlier, this experience actually occurred in parts. I have had this happen a number of times, where a visionary experience reoccurs and I am given more in the way of revelation about things already seen, or the vision takes on additional detail and depth.

It is a principle that once you have been to a certain place in the heavens you are able to return with greater ease. Now and again, recalling in memory or talking about an experience can open the way to re-enter, and sometimes to be taken further into it. But most of the time when I revisit a revelatory experience it is by the prompting of the Spirit. The Lord explained it to me this way:

> "Once you have received something that is part of your inheritance in Me, you then possess it. As long as you remain within my Kingdom it remains yours. All that I give you here is everlasting and has eternal value. It is not disposable or for one time use. You become more practiced and skilled in the things I give you with their use. So, you must return to things opened up to you in order to mature and find the fullness of what I have for you in them. So it is with visions that are beyond simple prophecy."

*Ps 89:14*
*Righteousness and justice are the foundation of Your throne; Mercy and truth go before Your face.*
*NKJV*

My initial thoughts on this experience are that the sea of glass did not actually lose its solid form, but I was being immersed, or baptized, into it. The foundation of the Lord's Throne is immovable and solid. But we can be immersed into mercy and truth. Looking deep into the truth (that is the Lord who is Truth) comes as we plunge deeper into the revelation of our right relationship with Him and then embrace and live by the truth that we are given. Greater dimensions of revelation in truth and advancement in righteousness are opened up to us as we look intently into these things and come into conformity with what we see there.

The foundation of God's Throne is righteousness and justice. The sea of glass is perfectly peaceful and a symbol of His truth and mercy. Because He has made truth available without limit in His mercy, His judgments are righteous. His authority and rule are based on absolute truth, justice, mercy and right action in every regard, without fail. Eternal perfect peace, tranquility, and clarity are the results of living in accordance with these things.

I did not leave my body and had awareness of it during the entire vision. I was able to open my physical eyes and see my natural surroundings. With my eyes open I was still able to perceive the vision, but in less detail and it seemed fainter. If the phone would have rung I would have heard it and been drawn out of the vision.

These visits to the Throne Room were no where near the level of encounter that John had during the Revelation of Jesus Christ. Even though I went to the same place, I was not completely "caught up" the way that John was. I did not see the living creatures or elders or any angels during this visit. There were other differences as well.

Even though we may be brought into a heavenly place that others before us have visited does not mean that we will have the same experience they did. For instance, John was certainly familiar with the prophet Ezekiel's Throne Room encounter before he received the Revelation. There are some striking similarities between Ezekiel 1 and Revelation 4.

There are also many things that differ in the two accounts. Ezekiel saw, and heard things that John did not and vice versa. You are not limited to what another may experience in the heavens, nor does it diminish the legitimacy of your encounter, should you not experience every detail of another's vision.

## How to activate visits in the Heavenly Places

Meditating on the passages of the Bible that document visions of God[69] is a good way to prepare yourself for third heaven experiences of your own. I imagine this was one thing that helped prepare John for the visions of Revelation.

Visions and glory realm visits where one loses awareness of their body and surroundings completely, are far less frequent than the type of vision I just described. Most people will have less intense encounters initially, and progress into more vivid and detailed experiences. This has to do with the development of our spiritual senses, but is also a matter of the sovereign will of God. Glory realm encounters come at the behest of the Father. We do not initiate them ourselves, though we can earnestly desire and seek God for them.

We have spiritual senses just as we have natural senses. We must develop our spiritual senses so that they become more acute. Praying in tongues, fasting, meditating on Scripture and prayer all help in developing spiritual sensitivity. When the spirit becomes strong and dominates over the mind, emotions and body, we are able to perceive with our spiritual senses more readily.

To help you develop your spiritual eyes, you might try some exercises. Listening to anointed music that is conducive to meditating on the Lord and bringing you into the secret place with Him can be a powerful aid in helping to quiet the mind and body. Be sure that your mind is cleansed and that you have dealt with any sin issues or areas of disobedience before asking for dreams or visions.

The imagination was created in us by God as the place where He can show us things. With a cleaned up imagination, or "vision center," we can be assured that what is seen there is from the Lord. Before seeking visions, dreams, prophetic words, third heaven experiences, etc, ask God to reveal anything you may need to correct and do what He may tell you. You must keep your thought life pure to prepare a place for the Holy Spirit to show you things. If the temple of your mind is unclean, then you may not perceive things in the spirit accurately, and may even give entrance to deceiving spirits.

---

[69] The accounts of those who "saw" the glory of God are called the Theophanies.

So, when you have quieted your mind, and have entered into a place of peace in the Lord's presence ask Him to show you something. If you see an image in your mind that persists, it is likely from the Lord. It may seem small or faint at first. Try to focus on it and ask the Lord about it. Notice whatever details you can and then ask Him questions about their meaning. God wants to be engaged and He uses visions and visionary experiences to draw us into relationship with Him. He wants us to query Him about the things He shows us. When we do, He will give us more. Sometimes the vision or experience we are having will become more detailed and vivid, or take on greater depth as we ask and then carefully listen for understanding about what He is showing us.

As you progress in this, you will be able to see faint images or visions with your eyes open as well. Remember to focus and keep the Lord engaged, asking and listening for interpretation of what He shows you. The more practiced you become at this the more vivid your open eye spiritual vision will become. Soon you will be able to see into the spirit realm and perceive angelic activity at times.

Be sure to steward what He gives you well. Write the details in a journal and continue to seek the Lord for more understanding as you review your journal entries. Be patient, as God does not always give the interpretation and application of what He shows you immediately, at least not in fullness.

Your spiritual senses of hearing, smell, taste, and touch are also developed in similar fashion. Most people are visually oriented and will find it easiest to begin with their spiritual vision.

Sometimes people will have evil spiritual forces keeping them "blind." Addressing any areas of sin, judgments, unforgiveness, etc., first will make it easier to send those little pests packing.

Prayer from someone who has keen spiritual vision to help open the spiritual eyes of another can be very helpful. We have found it effective in helping others begin to see in the spirit, and have more godly dreams and visions, by laying hands on them and praying for their eyes to be opened. Again, this should only be done with those who are maintaining a pure heart and walk with the Lord. Exercises to develop the spiritual senses are still important. People don't usually start having open eye visions immediately, but prayer can help remove hindrances to the development of their spiritual eyes.

## Realms of Glory ☼ 6 - Heavenly Places

Some of the hindrances to entering into heavenly places are doubt, unbelief, fear, and preconceived ideas or rigid expectations. You must maintain an attitude of trust and faith toward God if you are to receive anything from Him[70], especially spiritual experiences. Fear, doubt and striving are the enemies to spiritual vision and entering into higher realms of glory.

You must also be careful not to put expectations or limits on what the Lord may want to lead you into. Rigid insistence on having an encounter with Him of a certain quality or nature will likely squelch what He would desire to bring you into. Experiences vary greatly in content, intensity, and purpose. Learning to relax into whatever the Lord leads you into and just enjoying whatever it may be will help you get the most from your visits in the heavenly places.

Striving, anxiety, fretting or trying too hard to "enter in" are counter-productive and will only hinder your entrance into the spirit realm. Quiet, relaxed trust in the Lord of Glory, and rest must be developed and maintained in the secret place with Jesus. These make up the launch pad for voyages into higher realms of spiritual experience with God.

We must also understand that we do not control or actually initiate visions, dreams or prophetic experiences. We can prepare ourselves to receive revelatory experiences and become more acutely sensitive to the Holy Spirit, but He is the one who actually determines the timing, nature and content of what we experience in the Spirit. It is certainly appropriate to place ourselves before Him in a posture of preparedness and anticipation, but we should not try to "make" something happen in our own efforts. As we become more practiced in flowing in the revelatory gifts and realms of the Spirit, the easier it is to enter into these things "at will". Again, this does not mean we're driving, but that we learn to flow and yield in the Spirit more rapidly and consistently.

I hope this helps you to understand the nature of heavenly experiences a little better. As powerful and amazing as my experience on the sea of glass was, I was not into the glory realm. Perhaps telling you about my second journey into the dark cloud of glory, and what led up to it, will help show the difference.

---

[70] Heb 11:6, James 1:6-8

**Activation**

Why not put on some good worship music that will help you to soak in the Lord's presence and come into His rest right now? Ask Him to lead you into a new experience with Him and to teach you to flow in the Spirit as you begin to explore new heavenly places with Him.

## Chapter 7
§
# Come Up Here

The motor in my pickup truck came to life as I turned the key in the ignition. As I reached for the power switch on the stereo, I heard the Lord's voice interrupt:

> "Son, I have much that I want to show you. Listen carefully," His voice came from within so clearly.

I answered the Lord with a "thank you" and left the music off as I pulled out of the driveway.

God let me know a couple of weeks earlier that I was to attend the series of meetings to which I was now traveling. My level of anticipation was high and I wanted to be prepared to receive all that the Lord had for me in the next few days. The Lord had been speaking to me about some things for many months concerning His plans for my life. When He brought this particular conference to my attention, He let me know that I would be receiving much in the way of revelation while attending. I was excited to go and also sensed the Lord's anticipation in the weeks leading up to this trip, as He let me know that we would be meeting in an unusual way.

Imagining that I would begin to hear what the Lord would say to me after getting out of Denver a ways, on my way to Kansas City, I began to pray in tongues and prepare myself. Only two blocks from home, it seemed that a veil just in front of my windshield tore open. It was like a torrent of revelation and prophetic vision rushed into the truck. I was taken by surprise and slowed down near the curb thinking I might need to pull over, should I be taken into an open vision. The anointing was incredible. I sensed the Lord saying that it was OK and that I should continue to drive on. This began a continual stream of remarkable revelatory experiences that lasted for over one week.

A number of times during my road trip, I received a word of knowledge or word of wisdom. While meditating on it and wondering if I was accurately interpreting what I had gotten in the spirit, on a billboard, or license plate or written in the dirt on the back of a semi trailer would be the words just spoken to me. Confirmation of some of what the Lord was saying to me came within minutes.

God also dealt with several issues of the heart during the ten hour journey. Even though I had been preparing myself in the secret place with Him for a long time, there was a deeper work of cleansing and healing that He wanted me to submit to. He showed me areas of wounding that required more healing and where I needed to release a few people from judgments I had made about them. He was stressing the importance of purifying myself in a very deep way to prepare for what He wanted to give me over the next few days.

The work He was calling me to in the coming days was a topic the Lord had been speaking to me about, as well. It would require that I take large steps of faith, and I wanted to be certain that my understanding of what I was hearing was accurate. He assured me that I would have no doubt about what He was telling me, before the week was over.

Sitting in a meeting two days later, I told the Lord that I wanted to see Him. I reminded Him of Moses and how he wanted assurance concerning the Lord's instructions to him. I spoke silently to Him, saying "Lord, if I don't see you and know that you have sent me to do the things I sense you telling me, I just can't do it. I need to know that you will go with me."

Not long after praying these things, a vision appeared at my feet. I was sitting bent forward with my head in my hands, and elbows on my knees looking down at the floor, when a small pool of clear water appeared. It was about two feet deep and had tan sand and rocks on the bottom. The voice of the Lord told me to put my hands into the water. It felt good as I rubbed my hands together and let them soak. "That's good. Just let it cleanse you," He said. The tangible presence of God grew thicker.

Suddenly, the pool of water vanished and I was looking down at a stone floor. It seemed further away than the pool had been. I looked up and saw that I was now standing inside a stone building. The walls seemed to glow as each stone was made from an odd translucent material. They appeared to be both natural tan colored stones as well as being similar in quality to gems. They seemed to radiate, or refract light of various colors. The light was not very bright, but quite beautiful. In front of me, about eighty feet away, were three arched doorways. The "sky" outside was purple and I could hear the sound of wind, as if it were rushing through a mountain valley.

I stood staring out the doorways and listening to the wind for a minute or more, wondering where I was and what I should do. Finally I asked the Lord silently where I was and what He wanted me to do. Just then, He appeared outside of the center doorway, and walked slowly into the stone building.

His face was radiant with brilliant white and golden light. I could not see His facial features for the blazing glory that shone from Him, but it looked as if He was smiling. His hands, arms and feet radiated intense bronze colored light.

He was wearing a white robe that also gave off brilliant white light. As He walked it was as if the fabric would tear in places and brilliant light would be seen coming through, as if His glorious splendor burned a hole in the garment. Then the opening would close and another would appear as rays of brilliance burst through the pure white robe.

I was completely astonished and couldn't manage a coherent thought. I remember wondering if He had come to meet with me or if I were just there to watch whatever He might do. Then I wondered if He could see me (brilliant, huh?). I was paralyzed with fear and struck stupid with amazement.

As I realized that He was walking toward me, I involuntarily fell to my knees and began to worship Him silently. Moments later He was standing before me and I was staring at His perfect white robe. It was beautiful. I was thinking "Nobody would ever believe that I'm only inches away from the Lord's robe, with Him in it!" My spirit was leaping in adoration and telling Him how much I love Him, offering praise and thanks for all that He has done and all that He is.

After a couple of minutes or so, I quieted myself to listen to what He might say. He was silent. I trembled. I continued to wait in awe for what seemed like many minutes, before asking Him:

"Lord, I am not sure what to do. I want to honor You properly, but I'm clueless. What could I possibly do to give you the glory you deserve? Lord, please help me. Let me know what the proper thing to do here is. I don't want to mess up or offend you, Master."

"You're doing just fine. I have you right where I want you," He said calmly.

Just moments later the scene changed. Again I was looking into the clear pool of water at my feet. Only now the sandy bottom had turned to gold. I wondered if the flakes and nuggets of gold were only a thin layer over the sandy bottom. So, I thrust my hands deep into it and scooped up hands full of gold dust and nuggets. For as deep as I could burrow there was pure gold, and not a single grain of sand or stone.

The Lord spoke to me inwardly about how He sees provision. There was great revelation of what has true value. He told me that provision wasn't a problem for Him, only for me. He said that I could return to this place to acquire whatever I needed to complete the work He would call me to. It gave me such confidence that I would never have to worry about Him providing for the things that He would ask of me, as long as I was obedient and moved according to His ways and timing.

This did not necessarily mean "prosperity" in the way that most understand it. Nor did I take it to mean having what I think I need, when I think it should be there. But only that God would provide what is truly needed in the moment of His determining.

Soon the pool of clear water disappeared as well, but the sweet presence of the Lord of Glory lingered on. I continued to ask Him many questions while giving Him thanks for such a wonderful encounter with Him. I wanted to know how it was that I was allowed to see Him in His glory and worship at His feet.

"What must any man have to see me?" He asked.

"Clean hands and a pure heart, Lord?" I answered in question, after thinking for a few seconds.

"Yes. We dealt with some issues of your heart on the drive out here, and I had you wash your hands before Me in pure holy water to prepare you for our meeting. Your prophetic odyssey has just begun. Our meeting in the heavenly cathedral has also prepared you for what is to come," He explained.

"Praise you, Lord! Thank you so much. What else is coming then?" I asked.

"You will see soon enough. Only keep yourself in My peace and presence and listen closely to My Spirit. Our next meeting will be all that you have asked for, and more. I'm looking forward to it even more than you are. I have been waiting for this time with you longer than you can imagine," He said.

I couldn't fathom what could be even more amazing and meaningful than what had just happened. The rest of the day and that night were wonderful as I continued in conversation with the Holy Spirit and drank in the anointing.

It would take many more chapters to tell you of all that happened during that week. But I wanted to describe parts of this meeting with the Lord to illustrate the progressive levels of glory we can experience with Him. Also we will refer back to this encounter later, in chapter twelve, to contrast the glory of the Son with the glory of Holy Spirit and the glory of the Father.

So, would I call this a glory realm experience? Absolutely! Though difficult to describe every aspect of it accurately, what I have written here should be enough to see some differences compared to other types of heavenly experiences. The most obvious difference is that I saw the Lord in His glory. There was a far more weighty aspect and power to His manifest presence as well. Also, the visions that I had were "open eye" and vividly detailed. While I could still see the natural environment of the meeting room with my eyes open (if I tried), the predominate imagery I saw was that of the vision. My natural eyes were closed during most of the encounter, however, making the immersion into the vision more complete.

As an act of His ultimate grace, and for no reason of merit on my part, the Lord led me through the process of cleansing and preparation I needed to be able to have this encounter with Him. My part was to obey and cooperate in being freed from all that He put His finger on in me. He responded to the great hunger and desire I have for Him, and even that is a gift from Him.

> *Ps 24:3-6*
> *Who shall ascend the hill of the LORD?*
> *And **who shall stand in his holy place?***
> ***He who has clean hands and a pure heart**,*
> *who does not lift up his soul to what is false*
> *and does not swear deceitfully.*
> *He will receive blessing from the LORD*
> *and righteousness from the God of his salvation.*
> *Such is the generation of those who seek him,*
> *who seek the face of the God of Jacob.*
>
> *Matt 5:8*
> *"Blessed are the pure in heart, **for they shall see God**."*

The following day, while in a morning meeting, the weighty presence of God became thick around me. I closed my eyes and was instantly traveling into the thick smoky glory cloud toward the very being of God. My spirit was soaring as the cloud became thicker and the glory of the Lord became increasingly intense. Billowy thick grey smoke and flashes of sparkling gold and silver light rippled about me as I soared further into the cloud.

Unlike my first journey into the glory cloud years before, I did not feel extreme terror. Nor did I have the sensation of vibrating with intense energy, although I was trembling. There was an immense sense of the fear of the Lord, but I did not fear annihilation, as I had in 1986. I was awestruck, but exhilarated.

"This is what He told me was coming!" I thought. As I soared deeper into the cloud the indescribable sensations of joy and peace enveloped and penetrated me to the core. God's love for me flooded my soul in reality and depth like I had never before known. The revelation of the grace and mercy made available to me in Jesus, manifest in this wonderful vision, was exceedingly humbling, heart breaking, and joyous.

As my traveling slowed I thought "No! I want to get even closer." I tried to "walk" or crawl forward toward what I sensed to be the direction of the source of all this sparkling smoky glory. The substance of it became so powerful and thick that it felt like I was trying to walk through wet cement. My strength vanished completely after advancing only a short distance and I collapsed in blissful stillness.

The cool sweetness of the thick vapor I was breathing brought back the memory of my first time in the cloud. I inhaled deeply and felt the invigorating substance of life saturate every part of my being. It was wonderful to feel the peace, power, love and life of God fill and change me.

I was transparent and could actually see the glory fill me as I took in deep breaths. I was aware of my transparency before God. The contrast between His purity and holiness and my fallen broken core fed the fearful revelation of His mighty justice. Even though the awesome sense of God's might and majesty brought the uttermost fear of the Lord, I was also aware of His complete acceptance and love for me. Each breath of the smoky mist seemed to cleanse and purge me to the very depths of my inward parts. I was being renewed in ways beyond my awareness.

I sensed His pleasure in having me this close to Him again. There is nothing that could possibly compare with the supreme euphoric peace, love and joy in that place with Him. Everything else faded into nothing, as He was all that was and all that mattered.

It seemed that the Lord of Glory, the Almighty creator of heaven and earth, had also made Himself transparent to me as well. No words can convey what it is like to be naked before the Almighty Holy God and lover of my soul, as He also let me gaze deep into His core being, in a place that only the two of us shared, wrapped in divine smoke.

The stripping away of the veil of my flesh and soul that had been accomplished by His Spirit, allowed for a far clearer view of His holy essence. I was being known by God, and He was allowing me to know Him. Communication between us was beyond the capacity of words. This transparency allowed for an enormous amount of bandwidth between us to commune through. Much of what was transferred between us transcended thought itself. It was pure mingling of spirit. Though my mind could not comprehend much of what was taking place, my spirit was overwhelmed trying to absorb the flood of pure holy revelation and glory.

Days worth of conversation took place in an instant. There was no possibility of misunderstanding or confusion in our communication. What He "said" or made known to me was crystal clear. There was no doubt about His intended meaning in any way. I was speaking with God "face to face".[71]

Strange things I cannot describe and have no understanding of flashed before me in brief visions. My perception of time became severely distorted.

I came to know a rest like none other, held safely in the arms of the Father. Confidence in my relationship with Him grew, because of His great mercy, love and grace. The sweet comfort and amazing acceptance He lavished on me were more wonderful than anything else I've known.

At one point, the Lord asked me:

"What do you want, Kevin?"

"This! Just this, Lord. I don't want anything else. I just don't want this to end. Who could possibly want anything else? Father, please let me stay," I exclaimed.

"You can stay if you want to, but your natural body will have to die. If that is what you want I will accept you into glory to be with Me forever now. Take your time and think it over first. I leave it up to you," He said.

---

[71] Ex 33:11

The desire to stay was strong, but I knew that would be selfish for many reasons. I also sensed that if I chose to live and fulfill God's plan for my life that my reward for all eternity would be even greater than this, though I was unable to imagine anything more satisfying. After thinking it over, I asked:

"Lord, what do you want?"

"Look behind you," He said.

I turned to see an opening in the cloud above the meeting room where my body was still sitting in a chair. People were on the floor and manifesting in God's presence all over the place. I thought that the glory cloud had entered into the room and that all of us were in it together, each having their own private encounter with God. I figured that no one was aware that others were in the cloud and that the Lord let me see what was happening in the natural realm of the church building.

"Praise God! Your glory has come. Thank you, Lord!" I said.

"That's not the glory," came the thought from the Lord.

"What do you mean? Look at them. They're all messed up in your Presence, God. Aren't they in the cloud with us now?"

"No. That is the anointing on the outskirts of the cloud of glory that you are in now. Some think that they have seen my glory and in reality have settled for the anointing. That is not the fullness of what I desire for them. So many think that they have seen it all and understand all there is to know about My Spirit and Presence and have thus limited themselves by becoming satisfied and losing their hunger for Me. Some would just want to enjoy the feeling of my Presence, rather than come in here to know Me and worship Me in Spirit and in Truth. They have mistaken my Presence for My Person. They either do not understand the price required, or are unwilling to pay it, to come here. I want all of My children to meet with Me here, but most of them will not endure the suffering and preparation needed. Their desire for comfort and other things is greater than their desire to know Me. Then there are many who do not know of this place. They don't know how I long for them to come to know Me here. I want to show them My glory, but I cannot while they remain in their current condition," He explained.

"Lord, what do you want me to do?" I asked.

"I want you to bring them in here," He said.

"What? How? I'm not sure how I got here, Lord. You brought me here. Can't you bring them as well?" I asked, more than a little confused.

"You will understand and know what to do in time. Will you go back and tell them of my glory and show them the way here?" He asked.

"Uh……yes, Lord. I'll go back. Please help me to understand this. I just don't have a clue how to even tell them that there is more, let alone help them in here."

"I will be with you. I will show you the way," He answered.

"OK. Thank you, Father. Please just let me stay a little longer" I pleaded.

"Yes. You can stay awhile," He said, sounding happy with my answer.

Until God prompted me to write this book I had no idea how I was supposed to even begin to help others into the glory realm. I know there is more to it than just this feeble attempt to express the fullness of what is waiting for you in God. God wants you to become a vessel of honor; prepared, broken, and purified; that is ready to reveal His glory to others. I continue to pursue Him and submit to His dealings in my own preparation to experience Him in greater measure in hopes of one day wearing His glory as a garment.

For about two weeks after this encounter I was exhaling the glory. The marvelous smoky mist I breathed in while in the cloud, saturated my being. When I exhaled a small amount into my hand and touched someone with it they either fell under the power, or entered into extreme visions, or they were delivered from oppression, or a few other remarkable things happened.

I yearn for the day when I will walk in this all the time, so that those around me who are in such great need can be touched by the glory of God in a radical undeniable way. It's the best way to make Him known to others. God's glory will be revealed in the whole earth. It's coming soon, and we need to prepare now.

Besides making His glory known, there were several other specific assignments that I was given by the Lord during this encounter with Him. All of what He had been speaking to me in previous days was reiterated and confirmed beyond any doubt. He assured me that I would be given everything needed to accomplish all of this. I had no idea just how soon some of that would come.

Later in the week I had another extreme encounter during a church meeting. The voice of the Lord thundered within me so loudly that I thought people around me might have heard it as well. "Stand up!" He boomed.

My first thought was concern over what the speaker and others would think if I just stood up in the middle of the meeting. I hesitated for only a moment before standing, as the Lord's voice was so clear and commanding. Once on my feet I started to raise my hands to Him in praise, when my right arm was seized and raised high.

I became aware of the presence of an immense angel standing behind me. The angel put something in my hand. He wrapped his hand around mine, holding it high. My eyes were closed and my spiritual vision opened suddenly to see a bright sword in my hand. I could feel the weight of it. I was unable to completely close my fist, as my natural senses convinced me that I was holding something solid.

"Open your eyes and look at your hand," I heard. My raised hand was held as if gripping something cylindrical, but I didn't see anything in it. I tried to close my grip, but was unable to. It was the strangest thing to stare at my hand and see nothing there, and yet feel the weight and the solid form of something in it. When I closed my eyes I once again saw the sword clearly.

At about this time I heard the speaker tell everyone to stand up and raise their hands to the Lord. He then began to tell us that he saw angels going around the room and putting swords in people's hands. He said that this was the commissioning that the Lord had spoken of to many of us. It was the granting of the power and authority needed to fulfill the divine assignments He had given us for the days ahead. Talk about instant confirmation! This was just amazing.

The blade of the sword was a brilliant sterling that seemed to radiate its own light. It was double edged and very sharp. There were odd characters and what looked like a Celtic knot design on the blade near the hilt. The hilt was brilliant gold wrapped with crimson leather or velvet strap. Intricate designs were carved into it. Molded from the gold and forming the ends of the quillions were the head of an eagle on one end and the head of a lion on the other. In the pommel of the hand-and-a-half handle was a large crimson stone, like a huge garnet.

I swallowed hard as the weighty glory of the Lord became even more intense. It was a fearful thing to wield such a weapon. I had a clear sense of its power and its potential to both deliver and to kill. As the angel gently directed my hand to become more comfortable with it, I slowly waved it before me with fear and caution.

> "Lord, I am not going to do anything with this until I hear from you very clearly about its use. Please help me to always respect its power and fear my own potential to work evil with this sword. I wait on you, Lord of Hosts, for your orders," I said.

"Good. That's very good," He replied.

He then explained to me that the angel that had delivered this sword would remain assigned to me until my mission was complete and I passed from this life. I knew this all meant that there would be some extreme warfare between now and then. I was fearful of what I would be led into. "Fear not!" thundered within me, just as I was having these thoughts. It shook me to the marrow and I nearly fell over.

Just then my left arm was grasped and a scroll was placed in that hand. The Lord explained that the scroll was my commission and it would contain my orders. From time to time He would write new orders on it and show them to me in a vision.

He gave me permission to open the scroll and read it. Apart from my name and specific commission, it was blank. I asked the Lord why the things that He had directed me to do a few days earlier were not written on the scroll. No answer came.

A similar situation occurred with a friend of mine. I was given a prophetic word for her and an angel came to my side to help me deliver the word. I felt the importance of delivering the word accurately and completely.

The basic gist of the message from the Lord was that He was going to increase the level of authority her words have in the spirit realm. She will be used to make declarations that will open strategic gates and call in provision to send small ministry teams into several nations. Her words will be empowered to make the way during times of peril when others would not otherwise be able to go.

When I finished delivering the word the angel at my side left me and went to her. I knew that this angel would remain assigned to her and was there to protect her and provide the muscle to work change according to the strategic words she will speak.

A few days later this friend of mine was awakened from a nap and sensed the presence of an angel. She felt something solid in her hands. It was cylindrical and seemed to be made of wood. She sensed that it was a staff, and her hands were positioned as if she were holding a pole.

This was confirmation that she had been issued a staff of authority. When she told me about this I recalled my visionary experience where I was given a sword. I also told her that I had the strong sense that the angel went along with the staff to bring authority to the proclamations she would make. Both would be there when needed.

It seems that when given instructions from the Lord in such experiences the time to carry them out is not always immediately after receiving such orders. Since this encounter with God, it has become clear that some of the tasks were for a time yet to come. Not understanding this, I pressed into some things prematurely. In His mercy, God blew up my efforts before I got too far.

Like me, my friend is still waiting for the Lord to show her how and when this authority is to be used. We must wait on Him for training and direction before using the weapons and authority He issues. Timing is everything, and we will find that we don't have the authority we may think if we step into things prematurely.

So, until I "see" the orders I heard actually written on the scroll given me, I will continue to wait on Him and prepare myself for His glory. You can't miss God by going directly for Him.

My thought is that this follows a principle I call "preview before promotion," or "foretaste before fulfillment." This is when God allows us to sample a taste of the promise. I explain this concept in greater detail in chapter eight. A brief description here will give it application to these experiences.

The Lord speaks words of promise, destiny and prophecy over us and then waits for an appropriate response of faith, thanksgiving and obedience. As we respond correctly, He then gives us a preview of the promises we are now hoping for. Sometimes we are allowed to walk in a measure of what is ahead, or enjoy a season of spiritual blessing and experience.

However, this preview comes to an end, often leaving the child of God confused. Disillusionment, anger, despair, and rebellion are a few of the negative things some respond with. Continuing to press into something that has not been delivered in its fullness is another reaction that can cause great damage to the individual and to others.

These previews are given to motivate us to press into the preparation required to possess our promises permanently. This is my current understanding of the encounters described in this chapter. Understanding this and knowing how to respond correctly is part of answering the call to "Come up here."

The wonders of these types of encounters with God are so vast in scope and depth that much about them will remain mysteries to be discovered for some time to come. Complete exploration of every nuance and every facet of the visions in this chapter would not comfortably fit between two book covers.

However, the more I come to understand about these things, the less I feel that I understand anything at all. The great mysteries and paradoxes we find locked away in the glory, and all the majestic wonder and revelation we are exposed to there, serve to make us so much less, and God so much more, in our sight. The more we see of His glory, the more we are undone.

**Activation**

Hungry yet? God wants us to develop a ravenous appetite for close encounters with Him. Just ask Him to prepare you for encounters with Him in His glory.

*Lord, I ask that You would increase the level of desire to encounter You in the realms of Your glory in everyone who reads this. Give them new experiences with You and teach them to hear You as You begin to speak to them in new ways. Give them more of You, Lord. Thank You for being so loving and generous, Father. Amen.*

## Chapter 8
§

# Undone

Throughout Scripture we see that those who encounter God in the glory realm are undone in His presence. Those who have close encounters with God continue to be changed afterwards. They are further undone as part of God's dealings in bringing them into closer conformity with the glory they have been shown.

Isaiah had the realization of the depth of his sinfulness when exposed to the awesome holiness of God's glory, and the fear of the Lord came upon him in a profound way.

> *Isa 6:5*
> *And I said: "Woe is me! For I am lost; for I am a man of unclean lips, and I dwell in the midst of a people of unclean lips; for my eyes have seen the King, the LORD of hosts!"*

Isaiah was undone in the glory realm. A degree of being undone is also pictured in the death of King Uzziah.

> *Isa 6:1*
> **In the year that King Uzziah died** *I saw the Lord sitting upon a throne, high and lifted up; and the train of his robe filled the temple.*

The name Uzziah means strength. Our strength must die before we can safely enter the glory realms. The strength of man cannot endure in the glory of God. Many times the Lord waits for us to abandon our own efforts and reliance on our abilities and strengths before He will show us His glory.

The loss of physical strength and an acute awareness of the fear of the Lord are common to these events as well:

> *Ezek 1:28*
> *Such was the appearance of the likeness of the glory of the LORD. And when I saw it,* **I fell on my face**, *and I heard the voice of one speaking.* [72]

> *Dan 10:16-17*
> *..."O my lord, by reason of the vision pains have come upon me, and* **I retain no strength**. *How can my lord's servant talk with my lord? For now no strength remains in me, and no breath is left in me."*

> *Rev 1:17*
> *When I saw him,* **I fell at his feet as though dead.**

> *Matt 17:5-6*
> *behold, a bright cloud overshadowed them, and a voice from the cloud said, "This is my beloved Son, with whom I am well pleased; listen to him." When the disciples heard this,* **they fell on their faces and were terrified.**

All of these men were already called by God and following Him. They had been appointed to "ministry," or dedicated service, to Him before they saw the glory. Their glory encounters were key events in being promoted or advanced in His service.

However, before they were commissioned God required complete surrender. The Lord had to empty them more thoroughly of defilement and self-effort before He could commission them into higher levels of service. They had to be undone.

Even after their glory encounters, these men faced great difficulties. In fact, you can bet on tough times after this level of encounter with God. Exposure to the glory often precedes intense

---

[72] See also Ezek 43:1-5, 44:1-4

trials. It is a common mistake for those who have experiences in the glory realm to misunderstand this, and then resist the dealings of God afterwards. Once our time on the mountain top is over, God will send us to be undone in the wilderness.

Moses was led down the mountain, after spending time in the cloud of glory, with a mission to deliver the Law to Israel. We can see that it was no easy task for him to lead the "stiff necked" people of God through the wilderness. God knew that Moses would need great endurance, patience and strength to carry out the Lord's instructions.

I believe this is why God chose to reveal all His goodness to Moses when asked to see His glory. The Lord knew that Moses' area of weakness was his temper. We see this earlier when he killed the Egyptian who was abusing a Hebrew.[73] Moses also destroyed the tablets of the covenant when he came off the mountain with God to find the people worshipping a golden calf.

It was Moses' temper that kept him from seeing the promised land for striking the rock in the desert twice. Moses misrepresented God to the people in his own human anger. The Lord understood Moses' propensity to become enraged. So, God soaked Moses in the revelation of His goodness to help undo this character flaw.

However the revelation of God's goodness was not enough to completely eradicate Moses' temper problem. So, the Lord tested Moses with the thing He wanted Moses free from. God sent Moses into uncomfortable and trying circumstances for many years to help prepare Moses and the Hebrews to enter the land.

Yet Moses missed it when he was so close to the promise.[74] It may seem that God's judgment was harsh. I mean, what's the big deal about smacking a rock?

The rock was a symbol of Christ, the Rock from whom living waters would flow. God commanded Moses to speak to the rock in this instance, rather than strike it. Moses misrepresented God to the people in his own anger, while God wanted to present a prophetic type of Jesus.

The water of cleansing and the Spirit that would flow through

---

[73] Ex 2:11-15
[74] Num 20:8-13

Christ would come as a result of God striking Jesus with the suffering and punishment we deserve, to satisfy His own Holy justice. Moses had fulfilled this prophetic act that foretold Jesus being struck for our salvation, earlier at the command of God.[75]

Later in Numbers 20, God told Moses to speak to the rock to depict the preaching of the gospel of salvation that would be made known to us and completed in Jesus. Moses struck the rock twice in His anger and rebuked the people when the heart of God was to demonstrate His great mercy to them, while also foretelling the great love and mercy He would make known to us in Jesus.

For man to strike the Rock of our salvation is a serious offense. Only God is the righteous judge who is worthy to bring such a thing upon Himself.

So, it is a grave mistake to think that one is perfected or raised above the possibility of sin by the glory. Lucifer was ever present in the thickest manifestation of the glory and fell because of pride. To keep us from entering into the same judgment as Satan, God uses both the glory and the times of testing in the wilderness to teach us obedience and humility.

We are changed from glory **to** glory. The in between times are designed to work out the deposits made in us while in the glory, to help us mature and take on more of God's nature. It doesn't all happen in a single visit, nor does a trip into the glory mean that we have arrived or become mature.

Paul was given a messenger from Satan, a "thorn in his flesh" to harass him after having an extreme glory realm encounter.[76] Like Paul, you will be buffeted after glory realm encounters to help keep pride from taking hold. It is not meant to punish you, but to purify and preserve you. It is for your further undoing so that God will not have to judge you.

While these extraordinary glimpses of the Almighty cannot be earned, there is always a price to pay for them.

Even Jesus was sent into the wilderness to be tested and to suffer after having heaven open over Him and hearing the audible voice of God announce His approval of the Son.[77] Just as Jesus

---

[75] Ex 17:6-7
[76] 2 Cor 12:7-9
[77] Mk 1:10-13

suffered in the wilderness, He also suffered and was opposed throughout His ministry. Yet, God was with Him. Just as He will be with you as you walk through the desert.

Jesus was anointed for His ministry, but did not go out immediately to begin teaching and performing miracles. He was driven into the wilderness for forty days to fast and be tested.

The opening of heaven and voice of God speaking words of approval and love over Jesus prepared Him to endure and submit to the period of suffering He was about to face.[78] Scripture tells us that even Jesus had to learn obedience through the things He suffered.[79] So, we can expect to face the same type of refining tests and desert experiences as well. We must be undone so that we can enter into the promise of eternal glory with Him.

Near the end of Jesus' trial in the wilderness, He was tempted by Satan to take the easy way to His "destiny." Rather than endure the suffering in obedience, He was tempted to end the trial and take what had been promised Him prematurely.[80] Yet, He chose to trust His Father and wait for the fullness of the promise.

If the call of God is on your life and you pursue Him in obedience you can count on the same tests. Just before the Lord is ready to bring your testing to an end and release something to you, the devil will be allowed to sift you. Satan will tempt you with the same thing he tempted Eve, and later Jesus, with. Satan will prod you to enter into your "destiny" before God has released you.

The only restriction God placed on Adam and Eve was to not do anything apart from Him. That is what the tree of the knowledge of good and evil is -- relying on one's own understanding and will to pursue things that look good; things that look like the promise.

There is nothing new under the sun and the devil hasn't changed his tactics all that much. The false god of "destiny"[81] is still one of Satan's primary lures used to get Christians to miss the fullness of what God has for them. Pressing into something before being anointed, tested, and released does not only cause many to miss their promises, it can also do serious damage to others. Stepping into a

---

[78] Mk 1:10-13
[79] Heb 5:8
[80] Mt 4:3-11
[81] More on this in chapter eleven

place of leadership or ministry can hurt others and lead them astray if we move ahead of the Lord's release and timing.

We have plenty of ministers in the church who are called, but pushed their way into position prematurely. Rather than wait for the clear direction of the Lord, they have presumptuously taken position and authority. Some have been promoted by man, but not by God. This is false authority and can only be used to serve the purposes of the enemy in the church. The Lord will be bringing correction in this area soon, and has even now begun to reposition those who have taken what has not been given by the Lord.

Jesus had to conquer the same temptation that caused man to fall before He could be released into His ministry. Expect the same and prepare yourself to stay submitted to God and determine now that you will wait on Him.

Just like with Jesus at the end of His fasting in the wilderness, and Paul with his thorn in the flesh, the devil is almost certain to harass you after coming down from your mountain top experiences. Part of the purpose for seeing the glory is to become better equipped to defeat the enemy. With each new level you obtain in your spiritual walk, the greater the opposition from the enemy. The kingdom of darkness isn't going to just sit by and watch you advance unchecked. You become more of a threat to the enemy as you grow in the glory. God will use the increased level or pressure and warfare for your growth, refining and training in battle.

The glory that remains on you after spending time in the cloud with God is certain to evoke a response from others. When you reflect glory it brings out either the best or the worst in people. Evidence of the glory on you will expose the heart condition of those that come close.

> *1 Peter 4:12-14*
> *Beloved, do not be surprised at the fiery trial when it comes upon you to test you, as though something strange were happening to you. But rejoice insofar as you share Christ's sufferings, that you may also rejoice and be glad when his glory is revealed. If you are insulted for the name of Christ, you are blessed, **because the Spirit of glory and of God rests upon you.***

Some will be jealous of you. It would not be uncommon for you to be maligned, slandered, misunderstood, opposed, envied and even hated once you have been granted access to the realms of glory. It comes with the territory and is meant to refine your character and burn off anything that would cause the glory of the Lord to break out against you.

Some in leadership may persecute those they oversee once the glory has touched their sheep. In any case, your response should be forgiveness and grace. Harboring ungodly attitudes will extend the time spent in the wilderness and will be increasingly dangerous as we approach the great outpouring of glory in the days ahead.

While it is common to be persecuted on account of the glory, it is important to guard against an expectation of being rejected for your spiritual experiences. Your expectations will surely be met if you cop an attitude. Blame-shifting or avoiding responsibility for something that may be a legitimate issue by claiming that others are just jealous or persecuting you for your superior spiritual maturity is a harmful trap. This can be evidence of pride, wounding, irresponsibility and immaturity. Openness to the correction of leadership and God, and honest self-examination before Him, are crucial to establishing and maintaining a balanced life.

The Lord will use persecution to work humility in you and to get you to give up your right to defend yourself. He wants you to lay down all of your strength and desire for vindication and allow Him to be your defense. Tribulation should drive us to find refuge in God's presence; in our secret place of intimacy with Him.

Give God thanks for these trials and embrace the suffering. Let them have their perfect work in you so that you will be changed into His image and not be disqualified.

*James 1:2-4*
*Count it all joy, my brothers, when you meet trials of various kinds, for you know that the testing of your faith produces steadfastness. And let steadfastness have its full effect, that you may be perfect and complete, lacking in nothing.*

I know, fun stuff, huh? I haven't always done it perfectly, but with each new round in the wilderness I endeavor to press into the pain and give God thanks for what He is working out in me. It will shorten your time in the desert if you cooperate with the Lord rather than resist and complain.

If you cooperate with His dealings, the wilderness is where you will learn to submit to God while resisting the devil. The will of man is there brought into submission to the Spirit of God. God allows the pressures of His dealings, the enemy, and others to rid you of everything that keeps you from completely relying on Him and seeking Him above all else.

While we are not to submit to the devil, we are to submit to God in allowing the attacks we endure to form godly character in us and increase our endurance. Discerning when we are submitting to God and resisting the devil, without submitting to the devil and resisting the work of God can be a worrisome dilemma, especially when in the darkness of tribulation.

Job certainly experienced this great confusion, yet endured his extreme trials without turning from God. Job got beat up because God was pleased with him. That whole story will mess up the "it's your lack of faith that got you into this mess" theology so many hold these days. A gospel of comfort and ease ignores the deeper dealings of God with His servants that He desires to promote above those that seek His blessings alone.

Though Job did not perform flawlessly during his tests, I have not met many people who would have faired any better. Those who press into God and serve Him with absolute devotion will be tested in many ways, just as Job was, but not likely to the same degree. Job pressed into the pain. Even though he did not understand God's dealings with him he had this to say:

*Job 13:15*
*Though he slay me, I will hope in him;*

While in a state of grief, pain and confusion let our attitude be as Job's. Let us trust in the great love of our Father, knowing that He will bring us through the night, even as by fire. Just count it all joy, as it should reassure you that He is actually pleased with you.

Another way we get out of synch with God is by mistaking a glory experience, or other season of spiritual blessing, for the fullness of a promise when in fact it is only a sample. This is a principle I call "preview before promotion," or "foretaste before fulfillment."

Often people will mistake the foretaste of a thing for its fulfillment or fullness. God will allow us to preview what He is preparing us for in a way that seems to be the possession of it. This happens in many areas of our spiritual life and at various times.

The Lord will speak words of destiny or prophecy to us through others, or directly to our hearts, to spark faith and hope so that we will come into agreement with His will. Once we have received the promise by faith, He will then allow us to get a glimpse of what it will be like for us when He releases it to us in its fullness. This preview comes after we have proven faithful and obedient to Him.

When we begin to grow in our love for Him and demonstrate our commitment to following Him at all costs, He will then grant a good taste of what is ahead. This may happen a number of times before we actually come to permanently posses the promise.

Abraham received the word of promise, but did not see the fruit of it until he first demonstrated faith, obedience and total devotion to God. Abraham was allowed to sample the promise, in Isaac, but had to wait on God for it to be released to him in greater fullness.

God spoke many words of destiny over Israel and led them out of Egypt toward their promises. They were tested by God. Not until they demonstrated faith, obedience and devotion to the Lord did they come to the place where God allowed them a foretaste of the fruit of the promise. The spies brought back the huge cluster of grapes and other samples of the good things waiting for them in the promised land.

This was only a foretaste not the fullness. It was preview, not possession. To live in the fullness of this, and to enjoy these good things perpetually, they had to wait on God, move into the land and war for their inheritance. If they had eaten the sample bounty and remained camped outside of the land, they would never have taken possession of the promises. Yet this is what we do so often with our promises, because we mistake the preview for possession.

This commonly happens at the beginning of our walk with the Lord. Some call it the "honeymoon" period, when the new believer experiences ease in warfare and may have dramatic miracles of healing and deliverance. The Lord's presence is manifest around them continually and they have incredible love, peace and joy. Revelation from the Bible seems to flow like a river, as they begin to have their spiritual senses enlivened and soak in the basic truths of the faith. They are shielded and protected from many of the trials that they will have to face later and may come to believe that they have been completely delivered from the effects of past sin and wounding. The honeymoon may last for a number of months before things start to change, sometimes coming to an abrupt halt.

While a honeymoon is not always the experience of the new convert, it is common. I think that it would be more common if more new Christians were given a proper introduction into the Kingdom, as I describe in chapter five.

The loss of the sense of His wonderful presence and the specter of unhealed areas and sin begin to surface as the honeymoon ends. Prayer and Scripture reading seem more difficult and less fruitful. Temptations seem to resurface and the struggle to overcome the sinful nature by the Spirit becomes more intense.

All of this is by design and will cause great pain and confusion in those who misunderstand what's happening. The Lord has given these new disciples a foretaste of the life He wants to lead them into and experience in even greater fullness. This is meant to give them hope and to bolster endurance for the battles ahead. The sweet memory of the intimacy with the Lord that came and persisted without effort is meant to sustain them as they go through the pain and suffering of war and growth.

The Lord will test and reveal to them the true nature of their hearts desire. Love of God's blessings and desire for the pleasure of His presence must be placed after love for God Himself. God wants to be pursued. He wants us to seek Him with all of our heart before He will be found. As we learn to delight ourselves in Him, and not just in His blessings, He will then form within us the godly desires He wants us to have.[82]

---

[82] Ps 37:4

God has revealed His unconditional love, mercy and grace to us in many ways. This should serve to keep us in pursuit of Him for clear understanding about our current circumstances. If we mistake seasons of blessing as the arrival of the promise when in fact it is only a foretaste, or an oasis given to keep us pressing into the pain of preparation, we will react in a way that will actually keep us from the fullness of our promises in Him.

God led Israel through the wilderness with a cloud of glory by day.[83] He brings us closer to the promise of abiding in the glory by letting us see it. We follow after the cloud when we are able to "see" in the day; when our spiritual vision and sense of direction is clear.

At night, during our times of darkness, when vision is limited and our view of the landscape is obscured, the Lord leads by fire. The fiery trials we face in the dark night serve to refine us and to let us know that we are on course. We must press into the fire to be led closer to the promise.

The fire burns up the things of the flesh in preparation for more of His glory. The yoke of the Lord is easy and His burden light on the spiritual man.[84] So, the fire is only painful and troublesome to the carnal man. Though the dark night of the soul may not be pleasant, God still leads us as we draw close to the warmth of His holy fire. He is our comfort in the midst of trials and suffering.

Day will eventually come, but if you turn away from the refiner's fire in the night you will be miles off course and further away from your destination. Don't turn back in the night. The fire of opposition and persecution is given to guide you along the way. It is confirmation that God is pleased with you and leading you through the dark times.

Obviously we must accurately discern when to continue a course that brings resistance and pain, and when to understand such things as "course corrections." Wisdom must be used, so that we don't persist in a path that is not by the Lord's leading. Blindly taking the path of greatest resistance is more dangerous than waiting for clear direction. The fire that the Lord leads by in the night does

---

[83] Ex 11:21-22
[84] Mt 11:29

not just generate heat, but light as well. Be sure it is *His* fire that is giving you illumination and direction.

Israel rebelled, complained and accused God of deceiving them by leading them into a place of discomfort; the Sinai. They presumed too much and did not respond in love and faith toward God when led into difficult circumstance. The Lord does this to reveal these roots of iniquity in us so that we can recognize, confess and be delivered from them. God did not allow those who resisted being refined in the desert to enter the land, as defeat in battle after entering the land would have been certain.

Many men of God paid for their extreme revelatory encounters with the Lord with their very lives. Isaiah was sawn asunder, John was boiled in oil before receiving the Revelation of Jesus Christ, and many of the other apostles of Christ were martyred. Ezekiel's wife, "the desire of His eyes", was taken by the Lord and Ezekiel was told not to mourn for her.[85]

God requires absolute devotion from those He allows to have such close encounters with Him. He will require those who are granted access to the realms of His glory to sacrifice things that would keep them from being completely set apart for Him. He is a jealous God[86] and will not share His most intimate friends with other lovers.

This does not mean that the Lord will take your spouse home if you see His glory, but it will come at a price. In chapters thirteen and fourteen we will discover more about the calling and life of the forerunner – God's elect who will lay it all down to lead the charge in bringing this age to a conclusion.

Asking for the glory will cost you everything, and more. It doesn't come cheap and must be valued and desired above all else by those who would seek it. It is wise to count the cost and be prepared to pay it before making a rash vow before the Lord. But the rewards far outweigh the cost.[87]

So, we must be undone in many ways before we see the promises come in their fullness. The greatest promise to us in this

---

[85] Ezek 24:15-27
[86] Ex 34:14
[87] Rom 8:18-19

age is that through emptied vessels that have been undone, God will manifest His glory on earth.

Is being undone the ultimate purpose in seeing God's glory then? No. We are changed from glory to glory. Our undoing makes way for the glory to have its perfect work so that we can take on more of it. Everything exposed to the glory is notably changed.

**Activation**

*Lord, help me to come to the end of myself, so that I might truly find You. Where my strength and ability ends Yours begins. Help me to see You even in the wilderness. I will choose to praise You and trust in Your love and goodness toward me, even as I walk a painful and lonely path at times. I thank You for the refining work You are accomplishing in me through the various trials I face. I rejoice that You love me enough to take me through everything needed to produce things of eternal value in me. I yield to You and give You all glory and praise, Eternal King of Heaven and Earth. Amen.*

## Chapter 9
## §
# Changed

While in the dark cloud with the Lord, He gave me some understanding about the effects of being exposed to the glory. This is where Enoch spent his days with the Lord, until he became so changed in body and soul that he passed into the cloud to remain with God. The glory is the substance and energy that transforms mind, body, and spirit into the image of Christ.

Enoch's old natural self was purified and transformed to the point that it was more like the atmosphere of heaven than of earth. Enoch was changed to the point of having his mortal being displaced by taking on incorruptible eternal substance. Finally, Enoch passed from the natural plane into the glory realms as a result. This is a picture of what I believe the body of Christ will experience in the last hour of this age.[88] Just like Enoch, our bodies will be forever changed in the final outpouring of glory.

The glory is the energizing substance of life, both physical and spiritual. The cleansing and purifying action of the glory changes us into His likeness. We take on the likeness and character of that which we behold.

*2 Cor 3:18*
*And we all, with unveiled face,* **beholding the glory of the Lord,** *are being transformed into the same image from one degree of glory to another. For this comes from the Lord who is the Spirit.*

---

[88] More on this in the last chapter

From the realms of glory, physical and emotional healing can be accessed on an entirely different level than by way of the gift of healing. An increase in the level of power and precision in the use of the gifts of the Holy Spirit follows exposure to the glory.

The spiritual senses are invigorated and sensitized, accelerating advancement in their use. Many begin to have more vivid dreams and visions, or hear the music of heaven more clearly, or have their sense of discerning of spirits heightened after soaking in the glory. The way we operate in the gifts of the Holy Spirit may be changed after quality time in the realms of glory.

Access to hidden knowledge and deep revelation of God's nature and eternal truth are concealed in His glory. I am not talking about weird Gnostic revelations that are just plain kooky. All things that we come to know and experience in the spirit realm must be in complete agreement with the Holy Spirit and the written Word. True hidden knowledge and wisdom will always glorify God and reveal more of His nature, ways and purposes. Overactive imaginations and false spiritual experiences will tend to draw attention to man or evil spirits and lead away from sound doctrine and theology.

The level of revelatory "data" I received, while in the cloud, was much more detailed and altogether peculiar from the gifts of the Spirit. While in the thick darkness of the glory, there was a knowing and seeing that went far beyond prophecy, word of knowledge or word of wisdom type revelation. Exposure to this level of prophetic experience heightens every aspect of revelatory gifting that one might normally move in. It produces a greater lasting flow of revelatory experience. The way we hear God is often changed after being in the glory.

Battle plans and strategies against the wicked one are made plain there. War is waged from a superior vantage point, untouchable by the enemy. Vision and revelation are vast and give great advantage to the spiritual warrior. Warfare done from this place is nearly effortless, and lots of fun. The enemy is decimated by those who launch strategic attacks from the hidden place of the glory realm.

This is why the devil expends so much effort in trying to keep you out of the glory. Once you understand that it's your birthright to live out of this place in God and you pursue it with complete abandon, it is inevitable that you will find yourself in the glory realm, if you persevere. The way we wage war is changed in the glory.

In the glory realm prayer is very precise and empowered, as the wisdom to offer up the most effective supplication becomes nearly automatic. There is no doubt that the Lord hears you when you have such unbroken raw connection with Him. Things in the natural are more effectively changed by prayer offered from the glory realms.

Jesus was able to walk through walls and translate Himself from place to place because of the glory that permeated His resurrection body. The glory can cause the normal operation of the laws of physics, as we understand them, to be suspended or altered. Those who walk in the glory in the days ahead will find translation, open visions, and other unusual spiritual experiences commonplace.

In April of 2004 I posted a prophetic word on my ministry's web site[89] entitled "Glorious Pressure." It speaks about some of the changes that will occur as the glory of God is poured out upon the earth in days not far off. Here is a portion of that word.

> *Many people are sensing an increase of spiritual activity and warfare in the atmosphere. There is a sense of anticipation, and of dread.*
> 
> *The glory realm of God is bearing down upon the Earth and is particularly focused on certain cities and regions. As it gets closer the second heaven will be compressed, one result being increased demonic and angelic activity. The enemy is reacting as the forces of darkness come under increasing pressure. With less room to operate, some spirits will manifest in the natural and become more active on the Earth. We are caught under the pressure caused by this compression. The veil between the natural and the spiritual realms is wearing thin and we will soon experience the effects of its tearing.*
> 
> *The only means of escape and refuge is to enter the glory realm itself, each of us individually. It must be "called down" upon the Earth for change to manifest, but we must*

---

[89] www.brokenbreadministries.org

*"rise up"* in answer to the call to *"Come up here!"* so that we are encapsulated by it. This is Psalm 91 in action.

The experienced effects of God's glory will vary according to each person's heart condition. While releasing great light, power and love through some, it will bring painful correction to the hesitant, and destruction to those who continue to appose His will. Isaiah 60 and 61 will find their fulfillment soon.

Our prayers and intercession can have great effect on specific events, regions, and peoples. Exercising authority, in obedient submission to God, will bring increase in the release of the glory.

Even creation cries out in response. The Earth will begin to heave and vomit as the glorious light of God exposes the depth of darkness that man has put it under. It trembles at the presence of the Lord and moans for the sons and daughters of God to manifest His glory and take authority over the forces of iniquity.

Watch for increased seismic and volcanic activity, especially in unusual places.

As we are initiated into the glory realm and find our footing, some will experience phenomena as a result of what I call *"dimensional collision."* Time dilation and compression will become common experience. This is initiatory and will prepare us for translation and spatial distortion. Many will understand what it means to be *"in two places at once."* As the faith and authority of those chosen for these things increases, their words will be able to move and reform geographic features, literally casting mountains into the sea. God is helping a few to understand the mechanics of these things even now.

Nothing remains unchanged once touched by the glory. All things created will be dramatically affected by the glory realm as it collides with our natural world.

It seems that most people live under the tyranny of the past or of the future. If we are too heavily focused upon the way God has done things in the past, we subconsciously limit Him and will likely miss what He is doing in the now. Likewise, if we live in the future, always viewing our fulfillment as being something to be obtained, then we miss what God is doing in the now. We must endeavor to live in the eternal now, while learning from the past, and holding loosely our God given vision of the future.

We are event focused while God is process focused. We look to events as being the milestones by which we measure time, maturity, and fulfillment. God measures things quite differently. Maturity, preparation, and accomplishments are not gauged by time, though they occur within time. The way that we live in the now is what determines our level of maturity, authority and position with God.

This defect in our thinking is the root of much of our errant theology and doctrine. We view salvation as being an event that is distilled into a single prayer, while God sees it as the process of being saved through our transformation into His character, by His Spirit. We fail to see God in the mundane as we look for Him in the spectacular. We fail to find contentment in our present situation and therefore miss enjoying God in the moment.

The fullest effects and realization of these things are experienced in the glory. In the cloud of His glory time becomes meaningless and all things just are. The eternal now is all that there is when the essence of God is fully in your face. The Revelation of Jesus Christ received by John is a prime example.

*Rev 1:19*
*Write therefore the things that you have seen, those that are and those that are to take place after this.*

John's visionary experiences were not linear. They happened nearly simultaneously, as most things seem to while caught up in timeless eternity. Jesus told John to write what he had seen, those that are and that are to come. So, He was referring to events John had already been shown, but that had not yet occurred in time.

However, the only thing John recorded seeing at that point was the initial vision of the Lord with the seven lampstands and stars. At the moment John wrote this, I think he had already experienced a good portion of the vision and was trying to unravel it, to give it some sort of sequence in order to write the revelation. This would account for why the book seems to jump from one time to another and report things out of sequence.

The Revelation is not written in a sequential, linear fashion. It is helpful to view it as segments, or layers, that have been separated from the whole of what John received. These layers are laid out end to end in the writing, but were originally overlaid one atop the other, as he experienced them. Finding the places of overlap in the sequence makes meditating on the book of Revelation challenging, but fun.

I understand John's frustration in not being able to communicate his experience with full clarity, as I have had glory experiences where the things "said" or "seen," the impressions, and conversation, etc. do not seem to happen in a linear fashion. They all seem to happen at once, but there is a logical cohesion about the whole. The various aspects of the experience seem to happen simultaneously, yet they continue to happen. It is as if the vision is completely experienced all at once, but persists in some sort of state that is both static and dynamic.

As we learn to operate out of the glory we will find liberation from the constraints of the temporal, making all things possible for those that believe. The miraculous will become commonplace as we learn to move in the realms of glory.

While God created music for the purpose of worship, worship is not dependant on music. Music is only one of many things that can be used in the expression of worship. Worship is being overwhelmed with the majesty and revelation of what God reveals to us about Himself. The 24 elders and the angels in the throne room have the joy of experiencing this without end.[90]

Worship is the compulsory, automatic, yet inadequate response that expresses wonder and amazement from experiencing the ever unfolding revelation of God's nature, character and essence. It is to recognize and ascribe all glory, honor, power, wisdom and holiness to the Lord, as these things become so undeniably evident. Entering the cloud of Glory is to be enveloped in all of this. The thick glory

---

[90] Rev 4:8-11

is a place of rest and peace, but it also gives vitality and strength to fulfill the assignments of the Lord.[91]

As part of the encounters that Moses, Daniel, Isaiah, Ezekiel and John had in the glory, they were each given a new assignment to carry out. Daniel was given prophecy to write, as were Isaiah, Ezekiel and John. So, it is with many of the glory realm encounters we will have. They will be our undoing in order to strip us of natural strength and come to a greater knowledge of the fear of the Lord. This prepares us to successfully carry out the orders He gives us.

Peter, James and John were not given a direct command at the time they saw the Lord's glory on the Mount of Transfiguration, but were prepared for what they would have to endure shortly after, as the Lord warned them in Mt 17:12. The revelation of God's holy nature saps our natural strength and reliance upon self and makes room for Him to become our strength. The intensity of such an encounter with God is not soon forgotten and fortifies us with the confidence that He is well able to perform that to which He calls us.

My experience also seems to follow along with these, as the Lord gave me some instructions and confirmed them during the glory realm encounters described in chapter seven. This happens at times when the Lord wants us to have no doubt about the authenticity and authority backing the commission He gives. Without such revelation, most would not venture into the types of assignments given in this way. The entire course of our lives will be changed after encounters with God in the glory realm.

However, I don't think that only those who have "callings" of certain types are the only ones God wants to bring into the glory. The entire purpose of this book is to help prepare you for such encounters and to prepare you for the great outpouring of the glory that will soon be here.

While I think that the Lord wants everyone to enter into the glory realms and come to know Him more completely there, I see that there are chosen vessels that will have to endure severe preparation in order to carry the glory and wear it like a garment. Many are called, yet few are chosen. Even among us who God

---

[91] Mt 11:28-30

desires to bring into the realms of glory with Him, few will qualify by answering the call to prepare and "Come up here."

So then, what qualifies someone to experience the glory? Friendship with the Almighty, is the short answer.

## Activation

*Lord, I desire to be transformed into the very image of Christ. Show me Your glory that I might gaze upon Your beauty and take on the likeness of that which I behold. Teach me to operate out of the higher realms of Your glory so that I will be an effective agent of change for Your Kingdom in the earth, God. Be glorified in me, Lord Jesus. Amen.*

# Chapter 10
§

# Friend of God

Many consider themselves friends of the Almighty, but what counts is who He considers to be a true friend. His desire is that all people would come to know Him in the most intimate way possible. But the choice is ours. We decide what our relationship with God will be like at any given moment.

I believe that there are four primary things that will determine the level of our friendship with God:

- Desire
- Motive
- Obedience
- Preparation

**Desire**

Moses spent a fair amount of time in the cloud of glory with the Lord. Even after being in the cloud of God's presence alone on the mountain Moses asked to see the Lord's glory. If Moses was in the glory of God and saturated with it why would he ask God to show him His glory? What Moses was asking for was to experience and see the very essence, or core of God's being, not just the wonderful vapor that God's center produces.

When God showed Moses His glory He had to cover Moses as He passed by so that the prophet would survive. The Lord of Glory removed some of the cloud that covered Himself and revealed His goodness to Moses. God revealed part of His central nature to Moses. If He had shown him any more it would have killed the man.

Moses wanted to see the very most private part of who God is. Moses had desire. King David was a man after the very heart of God. David's one desire was to see the Lord of Glory in all His beauty where He dwelt, and commune with Him; to inquire of Him in His temple.

*Ps 27:4*
*One thing have I asked of the LORD,*
*that will I seek after:*
*that I may dwell in the house of the LORD*
*all the days of my life,*
*to gaze upon the beauty of the LORD*
*and to inquire in his temple.*

Paul said that he counted his own sufferings as nothing and the loss of all things as rubbish that he might know Him.[92]
These men desired to know God above all else. They had intense desire that was never satisfied. They wanted to know and experience Him in ever greater measure. To become the friend of God you must first desire to know Him above all else.

Many think that they truly desire God but they remain satisfied with the level of revelation and experience that they have and make excuses to justify the stagnant state of their relationship with Him. We are all called to come to know Him through meaningful spiritual exchange. God wants us to pursue Him with complete abandon before He will make Himself known to us in greater ways.

*Jer 29:13-14*
*You will seek me and find me. When you seek me with all your heart, I will be found by you, declares the LORD,*

Even though he had been called to the top of the mountain with the Lord alone, Moses wasn't satisfied with his experience with God. From the time Moses had his burning bush encounter, his desire was to come to know the creator of the universe. He was fascinated not just by the physical manifestation that God used to get

---

[92] Phil 3:8-11

his attention. Moses was struck by the awesome being of God Himself. Moses engaged God in conversation immediately upon hearing the Lord's voice, rather than letting his attention remain captivated by the burning bush.[93]

God loves to surprise and dazzle us with His awesome splendor and mighty deeds. Many times God will get our attention through unusual manifestations and experiences. Their purpose is to draw us into a meaningful exchange with Him, rather than just amaze and entertain us. As we respond to His attempts to get our attention correctly we begin the journey toward friendship with Him, which brings the release of even greater manifestations.

If our desire is to know Him above all else, then we can be assured that He will form the desires in us that are in accordance with His will for us.

*Ps 37:3-4*
*Trust in the LORD, and do good;*
*dwell in the land and befriend faithfulness.*
*Delight yourself in the LORD,*
*and he will give you the desires of your heart.*

Many people measure their walk with Him by the level of blessing in their lives. They deceive themselves into believing that God is pleased with them, and their relationship with Him, if they are not experiencing any major crises and have their natural and emotional needs met. They confuse prosperity with blessing and approval. They may go to church regularly, read the Bible, pray, tithe, treat others well, abstain from sins of the flesh, and do all of the other things "good Christians" should do. But they do not fervently desire to know the Lord in increasing depth and fail to grow in their first hand experiential knowledge of Him. Jesus calls believers like this lukewarm.[94]

If you have lost your passion for the Lord, or if you have never really cultivated it, I urge you to cry out to Him and ask that He make you hunger and thirst for more of Him. Living in Laodicea is

---

[93] Ex 3
[94] Rev 3:15-22

the most dangerous place you can be in these days. If you have taken up residence there ask God to grant you a spirit of repentance and a one way ticket out of town.

The most blessed state you can achieve in this life is one of ravenous hunger and thirst, as the Lord promises to fill those who desire Him passionately. The more of Him you experience the more voracious your appetite should become.[95]

Pursuing the *things* of God, or His manifestations, are often mistaken for pursuing God Himself. Many mistake His power for His Person. They are enamored and caught up in His works and blessings and not truly caught up in who He is. The difference can be subtle but is primarily determined by motives.

**Motive**

Moses realized that he needed to have the most complete revelation of the Lord's Person, not just His power and manifestations, if he were to have any chance of succeeding in what the Lord commanded him to do. More than just wanting the stuff he needed to get the job done, Moses wanted to know God in the most intimate way possible. Moses had the right motive when He asked to see the Lord's glory.

Many Christians today desire to see the glory of God, and enjoy the benefits of being in His household, but have little real desire to have ongoing dialog and meaningful exchange with Him. Others have not fully understood that a deeply satisfying relationship with God has been made available to them by the redemptive work of Jesus Christ. In either case, both the believer and the Lord are cheated out of the joy of our primary purpose.

We should certainly lay hold of and enjoy every bit of our inheritance, as it has come at such a high price – the very blood of God.[96] But our inheritance is obtained as a byproduct of loving relationship with the Lord, not at the expense of true friendship with Him. Many come to God and demand their inheritance be given to them because it is their right. "Lord, increase my gifting, my

---

[95] Mt 5:6
[96] Eph 1:15-23

anointing, my finances, and my knowledge. Give me more power, more authority, more this and more that. You said ask and it will be given, so I'm naming it and claiming it…blah, blah, blah." Yes, if you keep asking long enough you might just get it. But if your motives have not been purified what you ask for is likely to bring destruction upon you, and hurt others as well.[97]

God wants us to seek Him first and then these things will be added to us.[98] So that when we ask we will not be asking amiss. Too many people are anxious to fulfill their "destiny," or build their ministry, or business, or have their dreams fulfilled, not realizing that those things will all be brought to pass as an outflow of close friendship with the Lord.

Develop your relationship with Him and the natural result is hearing Him, growing in character, gifting, anointing, power, wisdom, knowledge, etc. All things are freely given to those who value Him above all else, especially above the blessings He has to offer.

Have you ever known people who claim to be your friends, but the only time you hear from them is when they want something from you? They call you when they need something and act like they are really interested in your life and wanting to get together with you. But it's evident that the real reason they bother with you at all is that they want your labor, or to borrow something, or want your money or your stuff.

When this kind of thing happens to me I feel insulted by the fact that my "friend" thinks I'm too stupid to see what their real motive is. I feel hurt because they obviously don't really value me as a person or as a true friend. They just want to use me or my stuff. Many times, when I ask these "friends" of mine for help with something they suddenly become too busy. Of course we need to overlook (not ignore) such minor offenses, but it is natural to take notice of them.

Many of us have treated God this way at times. We love and adore Him when we want His blessings and resources, but pay Him little attention otherwise. God is generous beyond what any of us

---

[97] James 4:1-6
[98] Mt 6:33

deserve. He continues to freely give to us because of His generous nature and unfailing love for us. But do we ever consider how it must make Him feel when we become too busy for Him?

To those who value me for who I am, and not what I have or what I can do for them, I am glad to give whatever I can. When I come to trust someone as a genuine friend I want to bless them. It pleases me to sacrifice for them. When their love for me is not in doubt and their motives for having relationship with me are pure, I am much more likely to give whatever they may ask of me.

After God and my wife, Monte was the best friend I've had yet. We enjoyed a great friendship and shared whatever we had between us. We never had a serious disagreement that I can remember. We stuck together and helped each other out in any way needed. Monte and I had great times together.

I remember buying a Hohner Chromatic harmonica with money I saved up over a long period of time when I was about fourteen years old. It was probably the most valuable thing I owned at the time. I met Monte a couple of years later.

Monte and I used to hike in the mountains of Colorado and would go missing for days. We would take along a few snacks, but mostly ate wild berries and fish caught with worms we dug up using just a wad of line and a hook stashed in our pockets.

On one of our outings together I pulled out my harmonica and started to play. Monte wanted to try it out, so of course I handed it to him. The noise he made with that thing sounded like cats caught in a clothes dryer. I still remember the big grin on his face when he gave it back to me about an hour later. Monte thought that harp was the coolest thing he'd seen since his first bicycle. He asked me where I bought it and how much it cost. When I told him the price I paid for it his smile vanished. He figured buying his own was out of reach.

That night as we sat by the campfire he asked to play the harmonica again. The hideous sound he made with it echoed through the hills like a dying elk. I tried not to laugh but couldn't keep a grin off my face as I gazed into the fire and listened to him huff away on that harp. Every so often he would stop and belt out a few improvised lyrics from whatever goofy thought was going through his mind. I couldn't take it anymore and laughed until it hurt. He loved it and I loved listening to him.

After performing for his audience of one for awhile, he ended with "Thank you and good night!" as he stretched his arm toward me to give back the harmonica. "Keep it," I said. Monte was reluctant at first but I was able to convince him to take it. The only thing I asked for in return was that he learn how to play it properly. He never did. But I got more enjoyment from giving it to him and listening to the silly "songs" he would entertain me with on our adventures together, than if I would have kept it for myself.

That's how God feels towards us when we give of ourselves to Him and spend time just hanging out with Him. He loves to go on adventures with us and to listen to the songs of our heart that we offer to Him. The joy it brings Him makes Him all the more willing to give us even the little things we may desire, that are in accordance with His will. He wants to give us His very best and we should desire to give Him ours. That's friendship.

I would have given my life for Monte, and I'm sure he would have for me. Regretfully, I didn't get the chance to try. Monte drowned in a lake near his home after falling off a makeshift raft when we were nineteen. He couldn't swim. My swim team experience and lifeguard certifications went wasted. I don't remember where I was that day. I just know that we were both in the wrong place at the wrong time. I imagine he's playing a harp of a different kind now. Maybe he'll figure the thing out before I see him again.

How much more will God freely give to those who love Him and who don't consider anything their own, but are willing to give Him whatever would please Him? He withholds nothing good from those who truly love Him. His devotion to those true friends is far more intense than we can imagine.

I want that kind of friendship with God. He has given His life to save mine. How could I possibly doubt His love and devotion? But I have, and I have failed to be the same faithful friend that He is to me. We all have. But He is long suffering and merciful, and will receive us with joy as we turn to Him with earnest desire for real friendship.

One of the traps many fall into is to give themselves to the work of God, while neglecting their friendship with God. They think everything is right with Him because they see His hand at work in their ministry, but have neglected to pursue the person of God. They may be operating in high level revelatory gifts (prophecy and word of knowledge) with precision accuracy, seeing the sick healed through their hands, seeing people come into the Kingdom by their preaching, and seeing demonic spirits cast out and things affected in the spirit realm through their prayers.

But the litmus test that will be used when we stand before the Lord will not be if we appropriated the gifts, power, anointing, and resources of God and used them effectively, alone. It will be the degree to which we have come to know God and have allowed Him to know us.

*Matt 7:21-23*
*"Not everyone who says to me, 'Lord, Lord,' will enter the kingdom of heaven, but the one who does the will of my Father who is in heaven. On that day many will say to me, 'Lord, Lord, did we not prophesy in your name, and cast out demons in your name, and do many mighty works in your name?' And then will I declare to them, **'I never knew you; depart from me, you workers of lawlessness.'***

Some of these are like the prodigal son, who demanded that his inheritance be given by the father. Though they use the gifts, power, authority and grace given by Father God to do these works, it is not an outflow of their friendship with Him. Their motives are impure. Their true desire is to find fulfillment in their own efforts. They have denied their Father the joy of partnership in fulfilling their "destiny."

This is original sin – to do anything away from partnership with God. Although they use the things freely given to them by God to accomplish these good deeds, it is according to their own design and desires apart from intimate union with God. As noble and spiritual as the works may seem outwardly, these are in reality the result of their own lusts.

*Isa 65:11-12*
*"But you who forsake the LORD, who forget my holy mountain,* ***who set a table for Fortune and fill cups of mixed wine for Destiny****, I will destine you to the sword, and all of you shall bow down to the slaughter, because when I called, you did not answer; when I spoke, you did not listen, but you did what was evil in my eyes and chose what I did not delight in."*

The Lord is speaking to those who pursue and find fulfillment in their "destiny" rather than in Him. They will be shocked when they stand before God and offer their works of "obedience" to Him only to be told that He never knew them. Their confidence and pleasure are in the things they accomplish for God and not in God Himself. All they have to present to God is their "good" works.

It is not what we decide to do for God, but rather what God specifically calls and empowers us to do that determine obedience. He wants living sacrifices, not dead works.

Destiny can become an idol; a false god that is pursued rather than God. I am grieved by how many people I meet who place their "destiny" or call above all else. They mistake the wanton pursuit of their calling or destiny for seeking and obeying God. When one considers their "destiny" to be their primary purpose and goal, they will then see everyone and everything around them as being something to be used to help them fulfill their mission. They devalue and violate relationship and forsake true love for selfish gain. The gift of relationship and the true purpose of refining through relationship are then sacrificed on the altar of "destiny." People are then viewed as tools to be used, and if they don't promote or benefit the misled person's calling and ministry then they are cast aside or ignored. It is a form of lust and selfish ambition.

This is not to say that you should allow unsanctified mercy to steal the plans and purposes of God for you. There are times when relationships can be detrimental to our spiritual wellbeing to the point that separation is best. It is a given that Satan will send some people to draw you away from the purposes of God for your life or to try to shipwreck your ministry. Love is always God's way, though this does not always mean you should remain in close contact with those who prove harmful to you. Careful discernment and divine wisdom are needed to understand the difference and know how to handle such matters.

However, to cast off anyone simply because they are not a direct asset to you or because they can't be used to support your ministry is a grievous sin. This attitude is rampant in the church today. It breeds suspicion, selfishness, pride and division. People who have given themselves to the false god of destiny will wrongly discern when others are genuinely trying to speak into their lives in love and with right motives. They will instead accuse the well meaning brother or sister of trying to keep them from fulfilling their "destiny." We must learn to love, value and honor those that God sends into our lives and receive and appreciate what He desires to impart to us through one another.

Entering the fullness of our destiny does not come by way of direct pursuit of it. This is a paradox that is critical to understand. If we pursue our calling directly we are sure to miss it. We will lean upon our own understanding and make critical decisions based on whether we think a certain path will lead us toward or away from what we perceive to be our destiny. If we don't wait and trust the Lord to bring things to us in the proper time, then we will probably produce a few Ishmaels, and possibly forfeit the fullness of His will for us.

This is not to say that we should not have plans and goals that will prepare us and take us closer to the fulfillment of our promises. However, we must remain flexible and open to God bringing a change in course at any time. He does not give us step-by-step instructions on how to obtain our visions and dreams all at once. This is to keep us in close relationship and dependent on Him.

Not everything that looks like the promise is, and not everything that seems contrary to the promise is. We must learn to properly discern when the Lord is calling us into something that may not seem pertinent to our vision, and when an opportunity or request for something by others would truly be a distraction from the Lord's purposes.

All of this perplexity is designed to drive us right back to God to seek Him for direction. He will orchestrate crossroads and tests in our lives to teach us to place our trust, confidence and hope firmly in Him alone.

God wants our complete hope, trust and faith to be in Him, not in our ability to bring His promises for us to pass. We must wait on Him and listen carefully to His voice for direction and counsel. Without exception, He will at various times, lead each one of us in a direction that seems contrary to the fulfillment of what He has promised. He will test that we trust that what He says is true. We must come to a place of brokenness that truly recognizes that He alone is able to bring to pass the fullness of His promises.

Abraham was the friend of God. Just as Abraham was told to sacrifice Isaac, so each of us will be required to lay our promises, dreams, visions and ministries on the altar. Many feign a death blow to their Isaac presuming that the Lord would surely not have us "kill" what He has given us. This is not genuine faith and trust, nor is it complete obedience.

In the same way, we must be obedient in the moment, just as Abraham. God clearly told Abraham to kill Isaac. When the angel came and told him to stop, Abraham listened and obeyed. So, we should not become rigidly fanatic about fulfilling God's will for us. We must remain flexible, connected and obedient, moment by moment.

All of us make assumptions about what the fullness of the promise of God for our individual lives will look like, what it will include and how and when it will come. To reveal where we are in presumption and have made an idol of destiny, God will direct us to sacrifice it all – and not just once. When God calls us to lay things on the altar we must trust Him with complete confidence that He will "resurrect" or preserve the things He has truly ordained for us. Whatever things are consumed are best left with Him, as they would keep us from obtaining the fullness of the good things He desires for us. The holy fire that consumes the things of the flesh on the altar also purifies our motives.

I am not saying that we are to purposely destroy that which the Lord gives us in foolish presumption. Wisdom and careful discernment are again vital in these matters. But to be sure, He will test out hearts in these areas.

May God have mercy and reveal where our hearts have gone astray in making the blessings and manifestations of God idols. Just like the father of the prodigal son, Father God welcomes all who return to Him in sincere repentance and a desire to have restored friendship with Him.

The primary purpose for all of creation is that we would come to know God in ever increasing depth. It is also the primary requisite to fulfilling our "destiny" and is the ultimate goal of our faith. Many think the ministry and works the Lord may call them to are their "destiny." These are not our true destiny. They are only a means by which God brings us into the fullness of our true destiny.

Our "destiny," or destination, is not a place, nor a work, nor a position to be obtained. It is a Person. It is to be transformed into His likeness, by increasing in intimate knowledge of Him, until we have complete union with Him. We easily lose sight of this as our focus is distracted from the Source.

He has called us to know Him in order to be prepared and empowered to do great things for Him that will make Him known to others. This gives us the capacity to know Him even more. The works that He calls us to should serve to work further refinement in us and reveal our weakness and our desperate need for Him to be our strength. Too many times we ask the Lord to *give* us strength, when He wants us to surrender and acknowledge our complete inadequacy, so that He can *be* our strength. We must yield and allow Him to do the works through us. As we cooperate, we realize that we are both an active partner, and yet, we are also just along for the ride.

So, the tasks He gives us to do are designed to drive us back to Him in even greater desperation. As we learn to yield and flow in His Spirit as He empowers us, we achieve true success and claim greater personal victories in God. If we break this cycle we become ineffective and lose intimacy with the Lord, and therefore miss our "destiny."

Moses understood this. He didn't want to just go back down the mountain without being equipped to face the challenges of the commission God gave Him. This should be true for each of us as we prepare to embark on a new phase in our "ministries," or other new tasks He gives us to complete. We need fresh revelation of who God is and who He wants to be for us and in us at the beginning of each new season He ordains. It is out of our intimate knowledge of Him that we also appropriate all provision and the endowments of power, gifting, anointing and whatever else is needed to complete the mission ahead.

*Matt 6:33*
*But seek first the kingdom of God and his righteousness, and all these things will be added to you.*

Righteousness is the working out of God's specific and unique will for each of us by having personal knowledge and revelation of Him through deep intimate relationship. Jesus said those who desire this with intensity will have it granted. Again, desire and right motive are summed up in this verse:

*Matt 5:6*
*"Blessed are those who hunger and thirst for righteousness, for they shall be satisfied."*

Desire and motive were not a problem for me when I asked to see God's core being the night of my first trip into the thick darkness of the Lord's glory. But as I stated in the account in chapter one, I was not at all prepared for it. Two things were lacking. The first was a failure on my part to completely obey God in a certain matter. Also, I was not honest when Ira asked me what I wanted from God. I realized how stupid it was as Ira smirked at me just before delivering the "death blow" with a wave of his hand. I feared what Ira and the people there might think of me, rather than fearing God. Bad move. I now understand just how important obedience is to ensuring survival of glory encounters.

The second thing lacking was preparation, which we will consider later in this chapter and in the next.

## Obedience

*John 15:14*
*" You are my friends if you do what I command you."*

Jesus was very clear in His teaching concerning obedience to the Word and will of God. We cannot be friends of God if we don't do what He commands. Obedience is not optional if we are to inherit everlasting life and enter the Kingdom of Heaven.[99]

So many people these days call Him Lord, but do not consistently do what He has commanded in His Word.[100] This is the lawlessness prophesied by the Lord to occur in the last days.

*Matt 24:12-13*
*And because lawlessness will be increased, the love of many will grow cold. But the one who endures to the end will be saved.*

Not only are we to follow the Lord's teaching and commandments given in Scripture, we are also to obey the voice of the Holy Spirit as we learn to hear Him clearly.[101]

Even though Jesus was without sin, He had to deal with His humanity, just like each of us. He had to learn obedience through the things He suffered in the wilderness and in the denial of His natural selfish desires.[102]

Obedience is requisite to obtaining the promises of God. If Jesus was "made perfect," or mature, by what He suffered in order to posses the promise of His inheritance and enter into the fullness of His destiny, then we in like manner must learn obedience and allow suffering to work perfection in us, so that we might be transformed into His likeness. This is the qualification to progress into higher realms of God's glory – that we would become mature and holy, just as He is holy.[103]

*Ps 25:14*
*The friendship of the LORD is for those who fear him, and he makes known to them his covenant.*

---

[99] Mt 7:21-22, Jn 3:36
[100] Lk 6:46
[101] Lk 6:46, Jn 10:27-29, Jn 14:25-26
[102] Heb 5:7-10
[103] Jn 15:14, Ps25:14, 1 Peter 1:14-21

Suffering is a means used to ready us for higher levels of spiritual experience and access to greater realms of glory.

> *Col 1:24-29*
> *Now I rejoice in my **sufferings** for your sake, and in my flesh I am filling up what is lacking in Christ's afflictions for the sake of his body, that is, the church, of which I became a minister according to the stewardship from God that was given to me for you, to make the word of God fully known, the mystery hidden for ages and generations but now revealed to his saints. To them God chose to make known how great among the Gentiles are the **riches of the glory of this mystery, which is Christ in you, the hope of glory**. Him we proclaim, warning everyone and teaching everyone with all wisdom, that we may present everyone mature in Christ.*

However, obedience does not always equal suffering. The Lord's yoke is easy and His burden light.[104] Many things that He will direct us to do will be quite pleasurable. As citizens of the Kingdom, our lives should be marked by His love, peace and joy.

While suffering is not the only method, it is one that God uses to empty us of sin and self so that we might be filled with Him, in the process of preparation.

## Activation

*Lord God, I desire to become one of Your closest friends. Help me to purify my motives and create in me a burning desire to know You in reality. Lord, help me to be determined to come into absolute obedience to You. Show me the things that please You, and help me to see how I can be a friend to You and how I might satisfy the deepest desires of Your heart. Thank You for preparing me to come into even closer fellowship with You. I love You, Lord. Amen.*

---

[104] Mt 11:29

# Chapter 11
## §

# Preparation

The fear of the Lord is something that has been largely lost in the church of the early twenty first century. That, however, is about to change as God begins to reveal His true nature to the entire world in ways yet unknown. To avoid negative consequences, it would be best for us to seek to understand and walk in the fear of the Lord before He pours out His glory in greater measure. The fear of the Lord will produce the proper motivation in preparation for the glory.

> *Isa 11:2-3*
> *And the Spirit of the LORD shall rest upon him,*
> *the Spirit of wisdom and understanding,*
> *the Spirit of counsel and might,*
> *the Spirit of knowledge and the fear of the LORD.*
> **And his delight shall be in the fear of the LORD.**

When the Lord comes in His glory, His delight will be in those who have learned to fear Him. He does not want to frighten us off, but to draw close to us as we draw close to Him. Without the spirit of the fear of the Lord upon us we would not survive such close contact.

> *Lev 10:1-3*
> *Then Nadab and Abihu, the sons of Aaron, each took his censer and put fire in it, put incense on it, and offered profane fire before the LORD, which He had not commanded them. So fire went out from the LORD and devoured them, and they died before the LORD. And Moses said to Aaron, "This is what the LORD spoke, saying:*

*'By those who come near Me
I must be regarded as holy;
And before all the people
I must be glorified.'"*
NKJV

To offer profane fire is to approach the glory of God without the proper preparation and without the fear of the Lord. The attitude that many in the church today have toward God and His glory is much like that of the sons of Aaron. There is brash presumption that all who have accepted Christ can just barge into the Throne Room whenever they fancy and demand access to the glory.

God is longsuffering and merciful, but He is holy above all else. We need deeper revelation of the Father's love for us, but we must not make the serious error of ignoring His other attributes. God's love, patience and mercy do not preclude His holiness and judgment.[105]

If we fear the Lord, then we will obey and do what pleases Him. We will prepare ourselves by putting away all that does not please Him. Growth in holiness and character should be the normative pattern in our lives.[106]

*Hos 3:5
Afterward the children of Israel shall return and seek the LORD their God, and David their king, and they shall come in fear to the LORD and to his goodness in the latter days.*

In the latter days God will restore the fear of the Lord. Those who learn to fear Him will be shown His goodness. Remember that when Moses asked to see the Lord's glory God chose to show him all of His goodness. When we approach the Lord in fear and trembling, recognizing Him as The Almighty Holy God of justice, then He is pleased to show us His goodness.

---

[105] In chapter twelve we will further examine the standards and ways God has set for us to come into the place where His glory dwells.

[106] 2 Cor 7:1

A cavalier attitude toward the glory or an impudent approach to God, like what is so prevalent in the church today, will bring swift judgment when the glory arrives. Many have asked God to pour out His glory, not realizing the price and preparation required. They have mistaken the mercy, kindness and patience of God for His entire nature.

Some have said that we should just seek the glory and trust that God will not give us more than we can handle. The reasoning is that because He loves us, we can be secure in that, knowing that He wouldn't give us anything that would harm us. While there is a degree of truth in this, I think it comes from a limited understanding of the glory and of who God is.

God would not willfully expose His obedient and loving children to something that would destroy them, without first warning them. There are many warnings in Scripture about the various things that present dangers to us, but God does not prevent us from exposing ourselves to these dangers. There is grace to protect in some instances when one is ignorant, but not always.

The teachings about the awesome and fearful holy nature of God and His glory are made plain in the Bible. We must not ignore these things nor neglect the holy requirements He has given us.

The whole purpose of seeing the glory of God is to be exposed to His essence and attributes in a greater way. To presume that God can pour out His glory and just let us enjoy all the comfortable things we like about Him, while ignoring the holy requirements for coming into close contact with Him, is to insist that God do things our way. It is to reject who He is and to deny Him. How easily we forget that He is God (the name God can be translated as *Boss*) and we are His servants, as well as His children and friends. This thinking reflects the absence of the true fear of the Lord that so many have in the church today.

*Job 23:15-17*
*Therefore I am terrified at his presence;*
*when I consider, I am in dread of him.*
*God has made my heart faint;*
*the Almighty has terrified me;*
*yet I am not silenced because of the darkness,*

*nor because thick darkness covers my face.*

We need to accept, honor, and glorify God for *all* that He is, not just the things we like about Him or are comfortable with. We must stop creating God in the image we desire for Him to be, and humbly seek to know Him in reality. As we come to honor, appreciate and fear Him for who He truly is, then He is able to show us His glory and goodness without harm to us. The fear of the Lord will motivate us to live according to the standards of preparation He mandates.

In chapters thirteen and fourteen I will be discussing more on the nature of the glory and what causes God "to break out against" some who come into contact with it. For obvious reasons, these are important concepts to understand.

*Ps 24:3-10*
*Who shall ascend the hill of the LORD?*
*And who shall stand in his holy place?*
*He who has clean hands and a pure heart,*
*who does not lift up his soul to what is false*
*and does not swear deceitfully.*
*He will receive blessing from the LORD*
*and righteousness from the God of his salvation.*
*Such is the generation of those who seek him,*
*who* **seek the face of the God** *of Jacob.*

*Selah*

*Lift up your heads, O gates!*
*And be lifted up, O ancient doors,*
***that the King of glory may come in.***
*Who is this King of glory?*
*The LORD, strong and mighty,*
*the LORD, mighty in battle!*
*Lift up your heads, O gates!*
*And lift them up, O ancient doors,*
*that the King of glory may come in.*

## Realms of Glory ☼ 11 – Preparation

*Who is this King of glory?*
*The LORD of hosts,*
*he is the King of glory!*

The closer we get to the Lord and the more we see of His glory, the higher the standard of obedience and the more severe judgment becomes. Things that the Lord may have tolerated during times when we were less mature can get us killed, or even cause us to lose eternal life, after we partake of greater realms of glory. It is no small thing to turn away from the living God after seeing Him in His glory.[107]

The closer we get to Him, the more narrow our way becomes and the stricter our boundaries. This is why the fear of the Lord is so essential and something that we must grow in as we progress in our relationship with Him. God is gracious to pour out a heavy dose of His holy fear when we come into close contact with Him. This is not meant to scare us off, but to keep us from putting ourselves in a position where He breaks out against us in judgment.

Asking for the glory is no little thing. We sing songs about it and ask Him to show us His glory. In His mercy He has not answered most of those petitions. If He had come in His glory in answer to our requests, many of us would not be living on this planet right now.

So, let's look at some of the specific ways in which we should prepare ourselves for the glory, both individually and corporately as the Body of Christ.

*Luke 5:33-39*
*And they said to him, "The disciples of John fast often and offer prayers, and so do the disciples of the Pharisees, but yours eat and drink." And Jesus said to them, "Can you make wedding guests fast while the bridegroom is with them? The days will come when the bridegroom is taken away from them, and then they will fast in those days." He also told them a parable: "No one tears a piece from a new garment and puts it on an old garment. If he does, he*

---

[107] Heb 6:4-8

*will tear the new, and the piece from the new will not match the old. And no one puts new wine into old wineskins. If he does, the new wine will burst the skins and it will be spilled, and the skins will be destroyed. But new wine must be put into fresh wineskins. And no one after drinking old wine desires new, for he says, 'The old is good.'"*

The Lord used this metaphoric language to address the issue of fasting. Yet this passage has been used as the foundation for teachings that have led some segments of the church off track. To help avoid making errors in interpretation, we'll look at some basic principles to use when considering this passages application.

Whenever the Lord speaks in Scripture, either in the red letters of the New Testament or through the prophets of the Old Testament, His intended meaning is never one dimensional, but always monolithic. What I mean is, there are layers of revelation in the very words of God, and the truth will not be contradicted by the unveiling of additional revelation, but will be supported by it. The words of God are multifaceted in meaning and infinite in depth. There will be more revelation to discover from the written Word of God for all of eternity.

However the layers of truth locked up in the written words of God will be in agreement with each other and one layer of revelation will always build upon another. Truth is eternal and unchanging, while revelation is progressive.[108]

So, we must carefully apply sound hermeneutics (methods of interpreting the various literary forms of Scripture) to avoid deriving meanings contrary to what was actually intended by God. Missing the intended meaning of this passage then may well lead us off track and turn our focus toward things that will not truly prepare us for what is ahead.

To see what can happen when we ascribe meaning to Scripture that is not in agreement with its original intended meaning, let's consider one way that this passage has been misused. Then a few

---

[108] Isa 28:9-10

pages later we will come back to examine the context in which it was used by Jesus to see how it applies to preparation for the glory.

Many teachings on the "new wineskin" have proliferated in recent years. In some of these teachings, the term "wineskin" is commonly used to refer to church government or structure.

However, this is not how Jesus used the term within the context of His response when asked about fasting by the Pharisees[109]. The wineskin represents a number of things, but I personally do not see any application of this teaching of the Lord's to church government or the ascension gifts ("five-fold ministry").

Further, I think that the church's focus has been on creating the proper structure and organization ("wineskin") to prepare for the glory and the coming of the Lord, while He has been calling us to prepare our hearts (*wineskins* as used by Jesus) instead. We will not be made ready by defining the functions of the ascension gifts and then figuring out how they are supposed to work together and what the boundaries of their authority are, etc.

While it is of importance and value to seek God for understanding in His purposes for the functions of the ascension gift ministries, we have placed too much emphasis on this and taken the revelation beyond the boundaries that God intended. Christ is quite able to manage His church. He will not have the imaginations of man governing and managing the final episode of this age. Once again we need to find balance and seek for divine perspective on these things.

We will become one as we are one in the Spirit, not because we figured out what an "apostle" is supposed to do. If each member of the Body sought the Lord with fervency and obeyed His commands, then we would not have nearly as much division, strife, confusion and disunity active in the church. The work of the ministry would be done as each person sought the Lord to understand their part and then submitted to His Lordship.

We have made "offices" out of ministry gifts or functions. We have placed too much importance on part time job descriptions. These are not our "destiny," as so many have purported. These are temporal tasks that need to be completed to bring this age to a close

---

[109] Parallel texts of this account are in Mt 9:14-17, Mk 2:18-22, and Lk 5:33-39

and usher in the next. They will pass away when the perfect arrives. Our call, destiny and position are in the glory, forever. We must set our sights higher and keep the glory set before us in view, not some aspiration to an "office."

So many people are going to war with others in the Body because they insist that they must be recognized and "released" into their "destiny" by man. If God has truly called, anointed and commissioned you to do a work for Him, then all of hell can't stop you once God releases you. So, don't worry about someone trying to hold you back, because they can't, at least not indefinitely.

There are times when others may try to hold you back, but sometimes you are restricted due to your own actions and choices. At times God will hold you back because you are not ready for what He wants to release you into. Honest self-examination before the Lord of your readiness, character, maturity, and motives will reveal the reason for not being released into your "calling."

The higher your calling is in this age, the more lengthy and arduous will be your time of preparation. Wise counsel from spiritual leaders or mentors should be sought before moving into new areas of ministry.

Complaining about not being able to fulfill one's mission because man won't give position or title is evidence that a person is not ready for what God is preparing them for. They have not understood the true nature of the higher calling. We pursue the higher things of God by going lower. We must decrease, and He must increase, as we become emptied of selfish ambition and pride.

This is not to say that leadership is not needed, nor do I suggest that apostles, prophets, evangelists, pastors and teachers have no place or function in these days. The problem is that most are aspiring for position in the "church" organization, rather than taking their calling and ministry function to the world. If you are looking for a platform to operate from then find one outside the building.

What God is leading us into in these days will bring dire consequences to those that insist on a title and jockey for position. When the glory appears on God's elect, there will be no doubt about who is called and anointed. Those who try to usurp or oppose this legitimate authority will find themselves is grave danger.

God does anoint and appoint leaders in the church, and we should honor and support them. Some are primarily called to train and equip others to fulfill their (the saints) ministry, but the church is largely ingrown and inwardly focused. We think that all ministry and ministers are called to operate within the structure. The glory is going to be found as we go to those who are yet without the knowledge of God.

Respect and submission to God's appointed authority and ministers is absolutely mandatory. As we are released into our individual ministries, we must not allow a spirit of rebellion or independence to draw us away from healthy connection in the body.

While we know that God is dramatically reforming the way church is "done" and reshaping its structure, we do not yet know what it will look like or exactly how it will function. To pretend to know otherwise at this point will only lead others to build new structures according to their own understanding. God will have to tear those works down that do not conform to His true blueprints.

The containers that God will fill with His glory in these days will be those that have not been built by human hands. There will not be one uniform type of church government or organization. Small home churches and larger more traditional churches will all have their place. Again, we must let Christ build and rule His church in all of its varied expressions and forms as He wills. Demanding that others line up with our concept of what church is supposed to be like will just widen the chasms of division in the Body that already exist.

Small groups and larger structures need to work together in unity. Independence, rebellion, competition, jealousy and selfish ambition will bring defeat to those who will not join themselves to the Body universal. The leaders in the current organized church must not insist that those who God calls to function outside of their concept of "church" come under their control. Those who are called to walk outside of the "camp" must not be independent or disrespectful to those inside the four walls.

None of this negates the scriptural principles of submission to true authority. Our concept of authority seems to be perverted in that we become unbalanced, leaning toward either authoritarianism or anarchy. Many have either viewed authority as needing to be domineering, and controlling or they reject any form of leadership and discipline. Often, people will leave a harmful situation, but then place themselves in danger by refusing correction, counsel and discipline. As we humble ourselves and love each other, God will teach us the meaning and practical application of godly leadership and authority.

True godly leadership and authority will help to disciple others in becoming all they have been created to be in Christ. Practical training in spiritual things, teaching, counseling, and discipline are all part of this.

However many leaders have abused their sheep and used them as tools to support the leader's vision, rather than equipping and supporting them to fulfill their own God given vision. True spiritual parents will make way for their disciples to grow and release them into their callings, as God directs.

The spirit of Elijah is now in the land to turn the hearts of the true spiritual fathers to the children and for the young generation of end-time warriors to have their hearts turned toward the new leaders God is raising up in this hour. Let us listen to the Father's heart and be unified in His Spirit as we yield to His will in these days.

So, it is good to recognize and honor the call and anointing that is on a true servant-leader in the Kingdom. A prophet's reward is only received if the prophet is received. This principle applies to all of the Lord's anointed. We need to love, respect, honor, and receive with thanksgiving the gifts God gives to us in one another.

Until the Body of Christ understands all this and lays down pride, competition, ambition, and need for recognition from man, we will remain powerless and irrelevant in a world going to hell on a rocket. Since this is not the Lord's plan, we can expect correction to come to help transform us into the glorious reflection of His nature that He wants the world to see.

Now, let's go back to examine the passage on fasting. If we read within the original context of this passage in Luke 5:33-39, we begin to see the depth of its true meaning and application.

On one level, the wineskins represent the old covenant and the new covenant. Fasting is in order while waiting for the promise. The promise of a new and better covenant is one reason that John the Baptist and his disciples fasted; to help prepare the way of the

Lord. While they have the author and finisher of both covenants with them there is no need to fast, but celebration is in order (eating and drinking). Once Jesus fulfilled the Law and returned to His Father, then fasting was again needed to make way within the believer for the fullness of the new covenant. It is also appropriate to fast to prepare the way of the Lord for His second coming.

An old wineskin becomes hard and brittle from the chemical reactions of the fermentation process. Putting new wine in an old wineskin would cause it to burst. So, the new wine of His Spirit and the newness of eternal life made available to us must be put into a new wineskin -- the new covenant. The old covenant Law was a tutor, or guardian, until the new and living way was revealed[110].

To try to live life in the Spirit while under the mandates of the Law without the atonement of Christ would destroy both the purpose of the Law and those who the Spirit would be poured out upon. The baptism in the Holy Spirit would bring judgment under the Law, if the righteous requirements of the Law had not been fulfilled.

So, Jesus had to complete His work of redemption to satisfy the dictates of the Law and create a new wineskin able to contain the new wine of reconciliation and life eternal.

Jesus comments that those who have tasted the old wine say it is better. He is speaking to the Pharisees and Scribes; those who preferred life under the Law apart from true relationship and worship to God, rather than the liberty and life Jesus was demonstrating and would make available to them in abundance.

In reality, the new wine is far superior. Liberty in the Spirit of Christ is truly far superior to life under the Law, or dead religion. This was seen in Jesus' miracle of turning water into wine at the wedding feast[111]. That story is profoundly prophetic. The wine He made and gave freely was hailed as better than the rest, and the best was saved for last. We can expect the new wine of the last outpouring of God to be the best on the planet since creation.

So, the wineskin also represents us as individuals. God cannot fill us with the new wine of His Spirit until our old hardened outer

---

[110] Gal 3:24-27
[111] Jn 2:1-11

man is destroyed and crushed in the crucible of suffering. Only then can He fashion a new wineskin that is flexible and ready to stretch and grow as it is filled.

Remember that this teaching was a response to a question regarding fasting. Fasting is one of the chief ways to reform our old wineskins into new ones; to work refining and purification which increases our capacity for the Holy Spirit and the glory.

Fasting strengthens our spirit's place of rule on the throne of our will. Denying our flesh and soul what they desire puts them into subjection to the spirit man, as the will yields to the spirit. Giving reign to our natural desires will quench the spiritual life of God within us and make us dull of spirit.

Overeating, or feeding the soul with material that does not strengthen the spirit will cause us to become spiritually desensitized. Our western culture is completely pleasure and entertainment driven. Addiction to entertainment, pleasure, and escape mechanisms are the signs of a culture and people in the last stages of decay. People are starved spiritually and will seek after whatever promises to fill the emptiness of a dead spirit and anesthetize an enslaved soul.

We know that the Lord created all things for us to enjoy, but their abuse and overuse will stifle the spiritual power within us. While there is place for eating, drinking and enjoying the good things in life that God has blessed us with, our culture has taken this liberty to an extreme. Bondage to the carnal nature is the result.

The western church is spiritually lethargic and blind to her own perilous condition. Overindulgence, prosperity and comfort have made her arrogant, selfish and increasingly sick in body, soul and spirit. We are the epitome of the Laodicean church.[112]

The Lord has been sounding a trumpet to awaken us from our deadly spiritual slumber and become alive in Him. Little time remains to prepare for His visitation. Too many in the church have presumed that the Lord's coming will bring joyous blessing for the church and terrible judgment upon those in the world who have not come to the Lord. I'm afraid in many cases the opposite will be what takes place in reality.

---

[112] Rev 3:14-22

The Lord is about to visit His church and set things straight. Many will be shocked by the severity of judgment that occurs within the church upon His arrival. The level of accountability we are held to is directly proportionate to the level of revelation we have been given. He will not judge those who have not yet *seen* the gospel demonstrated, while His "servants" remain sluggishly entangled in the things of this world. Those who have been shown the love and nature of God in reality will be called to account for how they steward the treasure entrusted to them.

The western church has arrogantly claimed that God needs them to spread the gospel and so judgment will not come to North America. We are blind to the prospect of having our lampstand removed in short order. God will not use a lukewarm self-centered church in His end-time purposes. We are close to forfeiting the fullness of what the Lord has desired for us. If need be, He is able to raise up "ministers" from among those who have been condemned and neglected by the "church," without our help.

At the time of this writing, many of the most powerful men and women of God that will exist in all of history, have not yet been shown who God truly is by the church. If the church fails in her mission to demonstrate the love, power and character of God to those He wants to reach, He will reveal Himself to them in another way.

Jesus is committed to purifying His Bride before He returns. He will use whatever means required to rid her of all the filth of this world. For some this will mean suffering and great tribulation. It is simple wisdom to submit to the dealings of God now and cooperate in His work of preparation, rather than to resist and face an even more painful process of purification. North America is no exception to this.

We must humble ourselves before Him and respond to the correction and warnings that have been proclaimed for many decades now. Time is short and He will not delay in bringing His purposes to pass, with or without us. There is no longer time to waste. The season of preparation is drawing to a close.

So, fasting and prayer are two key means of preparation we have to strengthen and condition our spirit while putting to death the carnal nature.

Praying in the Spirit (that is speaking in tongues) is also an excellent way to help in preparation for greater spiritual experience. It will serve to cleanse and empty your inner being while increasing your capacity for the glory. Keen sensitivity to the things of the Spirit and increased levels of anointing are also results of exercising your primary means of yielding to the Holy Spirit.

Soaking in quiet contemplative prayer with the Lord is also one of the chief ways to build your relationship with Him and prepare yourself for greater experiences with Him. Contemplative prayer is waiting quietly before the Lord, seeking only to experience intimacy with Him in His manifest presence. Prayer that consists largely of speaking to God leaves no place for Him to speak to us. We must learn to quiet our minds and focus on His wonderful character and attributes to be drawn near to Him.

Some folks have trouble with this at first, as they are used to being active in prayer and feel that they must be "doing" something for it to be real prayer. The most effective prayers of intercession or supplication will come out of contemplative prayer, once a place of intimacy with the Lord is established. It also makes warfare and getting prayers answered a lot less strenuous.

This is really the core of everything that we have been created for – intimate relationship with God. As we discussed in the last chapter, this is really all there is that is of any value in life. Without the consistent growth and development in our love affair with God, the pursuit of the glory, or any other spiritual blessing, is but vanity and will ultimately lead to judgment rather than blessing.

Many wonderful books on contemplative prayer have been written over the centuries. I will recommend two here; one from the seventeenth century and one from the twenty first. "Experiencing the Depths of Jesus Christ" by Jeanne Guyon[113] is a classic on the subject. Madame Guyon wrote many other exceptional books, all with a common focus on developing a deeper inner life with God. "Secrets of the Secret Place" by Bob Sorge[114] is an outstanding work arranged in short chapters that make the book ideal for use as a devotional aid. There are many other excellent books available on

---

[113] SeedSowers Publishing
[114] Oasis House 2001

the contemplative lifestyle and intimacy with the Lord. Every Christian's library should consist of more than just a few.

The written Word of God is vital to our spiritual growth and life. Diligent study and daily mediation on the Scriptures is essential in our preparation. Devotional reading of a few chapters of the Word everyday isn't going to give you the meaty revelation you hunger for.

If you have trouble with your Bible reading being fulfilling and bringing revelation, you might try some of these tips. Ponder and savor the words you read. Ask the Lord to show you something you can apply to your life as you read. Trust the Holy Spirit to teach you and lead you into all truth. Learn to wait on Him and ask Him to verify what you sense Him showing you as you learn to hear the voice of your Teacher. It is better to meditate on just a few verses and get some good nourishment out of them than to read several chapters and get little from them. Think quality, not quantity.

Every Christian should learn solid and sound principles of Bible study and methods of interpretation. This should go without saying, but many Christians (including many ministers) are seriously deficient and negligent in this spiritual discipline.

There is a famine in the land, just as the Lord prophesied through Amos to those who do not love truth over comfort and pleasure.

*Amos 8:11*
*"Behold, the days are coming," declares the Lord GOD,*
*"when I will send a famine on the land —*
*not a famine of bread, nor a thirst for water,*
*but of hearing the words of the LORD.*

We suffer no lack of words being spoken and written, but there is a serious shortage of anointed solid teaching and preaching in the church. Be choosy about what you feed on in the way of biblical teaching. Learn to verify if something being taught lines up with the whole counsel of Scripture before swallowing a good sounding message. We should be like the Bereans in Acts 17.

*Acts 17:10-11*
*The brothers immediately sent Paul and Silas away by night to Berea, and when they arrived they went into the Jewish synagogue. Now these Jews were more noble than those in Thessalonica; they received the word with all eagerness,* ***examining the Scriptures daily to see if these things were so.***

Goofy heretical teachings abound these days, and few Christians have developed the discernment and skill to recognize truth from error. We are tossed about by every wind of doctrine with little care or desire for truth and sound teaching. Whatever nicely packaged message that caters to the soul and carnal nature that's wrapped up with a few textual proofs passes for "good teaching."

Most bad teaching and errant doctrine come from taking isolated Scriptures out of their fuller context to support a hypothesis not supported by the whole witness of Scripture. Just about anything can be "proven" by taking select passages and claiming them as proof for whatever silly thing one might desire to present as "truth."

Our attitude must be to go to the Scriptures to see what they say and determine the original intended meaning. We must allow our thinking to be changed by what we find, rather than taking our ideas to the Scriptures and look for verses that support what we already believe. You might be surprised at how much of what you believe came from hearing the same things taught over again many times, rather than finding the truth for yourself by allowing the Author of the Scriptures to teach you.

We need to learn to feed ourselves from the Word of God by the leading of the Holy Spirit and by careful application of sound hermeneutics (methods of interpreting various literary forms of Scripture). If you haven't already, I encourage you to take a course in Bible study methods or hermeneutics. There are a number of excellent books on the subject and I have found one that is easy to understand as it is written for the average Christian, rather than theologians. "Living by the Book" by Howard G. Hendricks and

William D, Hendricks,[115] covers many excellent techniques that will help you get more from your Bible study and teach you to apply proven methods of interpretation. This will give you greater confidence in knowing how to derive the true intended meaning of God's Word.

I encourage you to check everything you read in this book against the written Word of God. Don't take anything I say here as being in agreement with truth, until you have studied and considered it for yourself. If I have erred in any regard in my presentation of anything here, I ask for your forgiveness and would certainly expect you to disregard whatever may not be in agreement with the intended meaning of the Bible, as revealed by His Spirit. The true intention and Spirit of God's written Word supersedes all other teachings.

Sound doctrine and growth in the knowledge, truth and revelation found in the Word will take you closer to the deeper realms of glory. All spiritual experience must agree with the sound teachings of Scripture. God's Word revealed by His Spirit and applied to our lives is of the utmost importance in our spiritual preparation.

Worship is also essential in preparing us for spiritual experience. It is the very thing we have been created for, and is the summation of all that God requires of us. Everything we do should be offered as an act of worship to Him.

Music is commonly associated with worship, but it is not the only vehicle we can use to express adoration and devotion to the Lord. Of course singing, playing an instrument, or listening to anointed recorded music that pleases the Holy Spirit and glorifies God are all excellent ways to help develop your spirit and prepare yourself for close encounters with God.

Worship can take on many other forms as well. Worship is the reverent, loving, recognition of who God is. Mediating on His amazing attributes and allowing Him to reveal more of Himself to you should evoke wonder and awe. Expressing this back to Him is worship. It can be done in many ways. Don't limit yourself to just a single expression of worship.

---

[115] Moody 1991

God enjoys it when we make an effort to do something special for Him to let Him know how much we love and adore Him. He designed us to be creative and it pleases Him when we find creative or spontaneous ways to worship Him. Just like young lovers who take pleasure in surprising each other with tokens of their affection, God is thrilled when we think of new ways to express our love for Him. It makes Him all the more willing to surprise us with special experiences with Him, just to let us know how much He loves us.

It should be unnecessary to write this, but sin in one's life must be dealt with in an active way before expecting to enter into spiritual experience. This will mean different things at different times in one's spiritual walk.

If we had to be absolutely perfect before the Lord would grant us any portion of our spiritual inheritance, we would never even get a taste. Out of God's mercy and grace He grants us encounters with Him, even as we are immature. While areas of wounding, defilement and sin remain in us, it is God's will to draw us close to Him. Without close contact with Him it is impossible for us to gain lasting victory and freedom. His presence and Spirit are the agents of change that purify us and help us to grow in holiness. So, the Lord is not going to withhold Himself until we get it all together. If He did we wouldn't get very far in our spiritual growth.

However, as we mature and claim more spiritual territory in the battle grounds of our flesh and soul, if we "backslide," or go back into bondage in areas where we have been delivered, the consequences are more severe. When we sin, we must quickly repent and make things right with the God, determining not to continue in sin and trusting the Lord to give us the grace to walk in the Spirit, so that we do not succumb to our sinful nature. It is this active resistance to our carnal nature and the evil one that is the outworking of the correct heart attitude.

Each of us is on a unique path of spiritual growth determined by the Holy Spirit. He will challenge us to deal with areas of sin and darkness as He sees fit and on His time table. If we cooperate and yield to His direction in the process of transformation and growth, He will withhold no good thing from us. Our obedience to His dealings and cooperation in being delivered, healed and changed into His likeness determine the state of preparation we have at any given moment. Greater preparation is needed for greater realms of glory.

However, if we compromise or take a lax attitude in dealing with the areas of sin and darkness that the Lord reveals within us, then we disqualify ourselves from intimate contact with Him and the good things of the Kingdom He desires for us to enjoy. We also place ourselves in danger if we pursue the things of the Spirit while in a "fallen" state. The higher we go in spiritual maturity and in the realms of glory, the farther we have to fall. So, we must be ever more diligent to maintain a consistent walk in the Spirit.

Attitudes of the heart and forgiveness are the central issues that will determine our spiritual condition and level of preparedness for accessing our inheritance in the realms of glory. A humble, supple, yielded and forgiving heart must be maintained at all costs. Love must be our prime motivator.

Jesus addressed these issues in *"The Sermon on the Mount"*, in Matthew chapters 5 through 7. The *"Beatitudes"* encapsulate the essence of the entire sermon.[116]

This sermon is really the summation and the heart of this chapter on preparation. Actually, it is the heart of Christianity. Careful study and meditation on the entire sermon that Jesus delivered on the Mount of Beatitudes, and finding its fullest application in our lives, is essential to maintaining residence in His Kingdom, and coming to know Him in all of His glory.

God is moving upon the hearts of His people in these days with a message of great urgency. He is calling us to diligently prepare for His coming glory. As we prepare individually and make ourselves a dwelling place for the Lord, He will then build for Himself a place of habitation in the corporate expression of His Body. When we have been shaped and fit together by the Master builder, then His glory will come to fill the temple.

---

[116] Mt 5:3-12

**Activation**

*Heavenly Father, I ask You to help me in preparation for more of Your glory. Help me to become more sensitive to Your voice and the things of the Spirit. Grant me a greater measure of Your presence and help me to make You the focus of everything I do, think and say. Take Your rightful place upon the throne of my heart and direct my way. I want You to be my one desire. Help me to return the love and kindness that You give me so freely, by pressing into the process of preparation for greater realms of Your glory. Thank You, Lord. Amen.*

## Chapter 12
## §

# The Temple

God is crafting a temple fit for His glory to fill, both within individuals, and in the corporate Body of Christ. He has given us a model for laboring with Him to that end in Scripture. The Bible's descriptions of the design and use of the temple portray vital keys we need to understand as we seek to enter the realms of glory. In this chapter we will see how the glory of each person of the Trinity relates to the temple and to our individual lives.

Father, Son and Holy Spirit are of the same divine substance, and exist as three persons, yet they are all one God. The doctrine of the Trinity is not something we will try to come to complete understanding of here (not that it would be possible to fully comprehend this mystery, in any case). So, as I describe certain aspects pertaining to the individual members of the Godhead, please understand that I am not trying to dissect, separate or define limits or boundaries around God. The assertions made about each person of the Trinity are meant only to aid in understanding how each helps to prepare the Christian and the Body of Christ for the glory.

There are several baptisms, or immersions, we must go through as Christians. The exact number and their purposes are a matter of interpretation beyond the scope of this book. However, I think that discussing three of them will help clarify their function in preparing us for the glory.

> *Matt 28:19-20*
> *"Go therefore and make disciples of all nations, baptizing them **in the name of the Father and of the Son and of the Holy Spirit**, teaching them to observe all that I have*

*commanded you. And behold, I am with you always, to the end of the age."*

Notice that Jesus did not say to go and make converts, but to make disciples of all nations. A disciple is one who is disciplined in the teachings of the master. Students absorb and process information, while disciples apply to their lives the teachings received, by coming into alignment with them.

Also, notice that Jesus said the way to make disciples was by baptizing them. Did He mean that dunking people in water should be the means by which we are to train them in righteousness? Certainly not. Recalling that the word *baptize* means to submerge and completely immerse something into a substance, it becomes clear that what He means is that one becomes a disciple by being completely soaked in the *name of* the Father, Son, and the Holy Spirit.

Jesus mentions baptism into each member of the Trinity separately indicating three different baptisms. He is not just referring to water baptism where the baptizer merely says the words "I baptize you in the name of the Father, Son, and Holy Ghost," as is the common practice in many churches today. *In the name of* means into the character and unique essence of the person(s) referenced.

So, the Lord was saying that we are to go to all people groups and teach them to become transformed into the image of God by immersing them into the character and substance of each member of the Trinity. We do this by first demonstrating the *name,* or character, of God to them by the example of our own lives. Then we are to mentor them in the ways of being drenched in the nature and presence of each person of the Godhead. True transformation cannot happen apart from total immersion into God Himself. We must learn to abide *in* Him, and then teach others in turn.

In addition to depicting being plunged into God, the baptisms associated with each of the three members of the Trinity are symbolic in a number of other ways. Baptism into Jesus is our first Christian baptism. We are identified with Him and agree to die to our way of life and live by faith in Him, as He gives us eternal life and the ability to fulfill His commands. It is the covenant made with

Him to enter into deeper relationship with Him by way of His Spirit. So, we then proceed to be baptized in the Holy Spirit.

Baptism in the Holy Spirit brings the indwelling power of God into the believer. God takes up residence in the Christian when they are baptized, or receive, the Holy Spirit by asking and seeking to be filled with Him. The initial outpouring and ongoing filling are essential to the spiritual growth and transformation of the Christian. As the believer grows in the knowledge of God, he or she is tested and led into trials for further purification.

The baptism in fire that John the Baptist spoke of [117] is for the refining and purification of the saint. I believe that this is also the baptism of suffering that Jesus spoke of.

*Mark 10:37-40*
*And they said to him, "Grant us to sit, one at your right hand and one at your left, **in your glory**." Jesus said to them, "You do not know what you are asking. Are you able to drink the cup that I drink, or to be baptized with the baptism with which I am baptized?" And they said to him, "We are able." And Jesus said to them, "The cup that I drink you will drink, and with the baptism with which I am baptized, you will be baptized, but to sit at my right hand or at my left is not mine to grant, but it is for those for whom it has been prepared."*

This passage is quite interesting. In answer to the request to be seated at the side of the Lord in His glory, Jesus asks John and James if they can drink the cup and be baptized as He will be. This is in reference to what Jesus would have to suffer to come into His glory. John and James replied that they could drink of the cup and be baptized as Jesus, not understanding what they were claiming.

The Lord's reply prophesies the things they will have to suffer to abide in His glory forever. He was telling them that entrance into the glory is only granted to those who willingly take the cup of suffering from God – the baptism of fire. Again, we see the path of

---

[117] Mt. 3:11

suffering and being refined by fire as requisite to entering the glory in the deepest way possible.[118]

So, the baptism into Jesus is in water for the cleansing of our sins, which then qualifies us and makes us ready to receive the Holy Spirit. Being continually filled with the Holy Spirit prepares us to be baptized into the Father; that is into fire for purification, in preparation to enter the glory. It is these three distinct baptisms that the Lord was referring to in Mt. 28:19-20 as He commanded His disciples to teach others to be immersed in each of the Persons of the Trinity.

Each member of the Godhead is also associated with a distinct type of glory. The Son's glory is radiant, brilliant light. We saw this in the Mount of Transfiguration event earlier in chapter two. The glory of Jesus that I saw during the experience in the "heavenly cathedral" with the Lord, as I described it in chapter seven, was also radiant light.

The Holy Spirit's glory is fire, as we see in the upper room on the day of Pentecost when tongues of fire descended on those gathered there. The fiery glory that appears on the outskirts of the dark cloud is also a manifestation of the Spirit. We saw this in chapter four in looking at the fire of the Spirit.

The glory of the Father is smoke. Smoky glory descended on Mount Sinai[119] before all of Israel, just as it did on the Mount of Transfiguration. It filled the temple in Isaiah's holy vision also. My experiences as detailed in chapters one and seven are examples of this as well. I was profoundly aware of being in the mighty presence of the Father while in the smoke during these adventures.

Now, let's consider the design of the temple building and see how all of this comes together. The temple was constructed with three primary areas. Starting from the outermost, they are the outer court, the holy place, and the most holy place. Each of these three sections of the temple building also correlate to each member of the Godhead, and their respective ministries.

The ministry of Jesus and His glory are seen in the outer court. The Son's ministry is primarily to the world. He is the Light of the

---

[118] Acts 14:22
[119] Ex 19:18

world, the Gate, and the only Way to the Father. He is the eternal Word that created all things. He took on humanity to make the way back to the Father known to us. So, we see Jesus in the outer court where He is visible to the world, ministering to the lost, the poor, the sick, and giving sight to the blind. It was in the outer courts of the temple that Jesus chased away those who had turned His Father's house of worship into a place of profit, merchandising and thievery, and called for it to be a house of prayer.

His glory of light brings the gospel of the Kingdom to the world and reveals the way to God. We are to represent Jesus in the world by being the light of God to those in darkness. He stands at the gates of the temple calling out to all who would hear, to come in and enter into life in the Spirit. He points the way to the holy place.

This does not mean that Jesus is relegated exclusively to the outer courts. He is seated on the Throne at the right hand of the Father, and is also seen in the inner rooms of the temple. So, understand that I am using these examples to help illustrate some important points. I am not trying to limit or place God in carefully defined rooms or roles.

The inner court is where the altar of burnt offerings was located. Forgiveness for sin is obtained here. As we enter in from the outer to the inner court by way of Jesus we come into the place where the sacrifice for sin has already been made for us.

Even though the sacrifice Jesus made is absolutely sufficient to eliminate the need to make offerings for the forgiveness of sin, the Lord still requires sacrifice from His children as an act of love and worship. The inner court is where we willingly sacrifice things so that we might not be hindered from entering into the holy place. So, the altar is still needed even though Jesus has already made the final sacrifice for sin. God will call us to lay things on the altar to be burned up so that we might enter into undistracted devotion to Him.

Between the altar and the entrance to the holy place was the golden laver. This is for washing before entering into the inner chambers of the holy place. This speaks of repentance and keeping a clean conscience before God. We must also release others from offenses we may be carrying here, and be washed from the stain of the world.

The holy place is where the Holy Spirit conducts much of His ministry. His glory is fire. We see this pictured in the golden lamp stand that burns with oil, and the fire that is used on the altar of incense. Everything in the holy place is covered with pure gold. This speaks of the refining work of the Holy Spirit's fire in our lives.

The incense represents ours prayers and intimate communion with the Holy Spirit. It is a sweet aroma to Him when we spend time resting in His presence in the holy place and adore Him.

The table of shewbread was in the holy place also. God commanded Moses to set the bread of the Presence upon the table often.[120] The Lord wants us to come and break bread with Him daily. There in the holy chamber of communion with His Spirit, we are fed and sustained by His presence. The spiritual bread of the seven-fold Spirit of God[121] is our sustenance. We derive our spiritual life and vitality from the Spirit of the Lord, and of wisdom, understanding, counsel, might, knowledge and the fear of the Lord.

Jesus gave this as a sign of the New Covenant with us in the Lord's Supper, or Communion. God's desire for us to come and partake of the spiritual bread of life, that is the Lord Himself who was broken for us, is made known to us anew in Jesus. The deepest yearning of His heart hasn't changed since He was moved to create the universe. All He really wants is to have loving friendship with us, and to be worshipped and adored for who He is.

The holy of holies, or most holy place, is where the ark of the covenant was. This inner chamber is where the Father's ministry occurs. His glory is smoke and it would fill the inner chamber when His glory came to meet with the high priest.

After putting on the priestly garments of linen and the ephod that was adorned with twelve precious stones, the high priest would stand before the curtain that separated the holy place from the holy of holies and wait for the appointed time to go in and minister to the Lord. The priest was not to sweat or do any work in the priestly garments.

---

[120] Ex 25:30
[121] The seven golden lamps depict the seven-fold Spirit of God as seen in Isa 11:2-3 and Rev 4:5

The white garments represent the purity and holiness we take on in the holy place by the ministry of the Holy Spirit. Work was forbidden to be done and no sweat was to stain the linen garment. This speaks of allowing the work of the Holy Spirit to bring about our transformation and purification. It pictures the requirement that we come to recognize that we cannot prepare ourselves or make ourselves holy and pure in our own efforts. It also speaks of ceasing from our own works and efforts to offer something to God that He has not called for. The only acceptable offering we can bring is to present ourselves in the garments of holiness and consecration that He has offered us, and to burn the sweet incense of prayer, worship and adoration to him.

Once we have been made ready we must stand at the veil and worship and adore Him until the time when He calls us into the most holy place where His glory dwells. The high priest would only go into the Holy of Holies once a year at the appointed time. Even after we prepare ourselves we must wait for the appointed time to be called into the inner chamber before the Father.

There are a number of stories in the Bible that tell of people meeting their natural end because they profaned the glory of God. Coming into the inner chamber or the Lord without the essential preparation and without the proper fear and reverence of the Lord can prove fatal.

God created man in His likeness, making us tripartite (having three primary parts), just as He is three and one. Mankind has a spirit, a soul and a body. These also correspond to the three primary sections of the temple and the ministries of the Trinity.

Our body is like the outer court. The Son took on a natural body and demonstrated the character of the Father and Spirit to us while on earth. In like manner, our bodies are to reflect the glory of the Lord as a testimony to others. We are called to demonstrate the nature of God to the world as we take on His likeness internally.

The soul of man consists of the mind, the will, and the emotions. This is the area where the Holy Spirit does His refining work. This is the holy place that needs to be renewed, and purified by fire. Once we have surrendered our will to the Spirit, we are then able to experience more of His ministry and take nourishment from the bread of His Presence.

The holy of holies corresponds to the spirit of a person. This is where we have complete direct union with the Father. His glory and the positive effects we enjoy from exposure to the glory of the Father, come by way of our spirit being connected with Him. As we burn up more of the defiling things that cannot go into the most holy place and bring ourselves into truer conformity with His ways and character, the more of the glory will flow from the spirit to the soul, and then finally out of the body.

The work of the fiery purification that we endure is a sweet aroma of incense to the Lord that goes up before Him. As we wait before the veil between our soul and spirit, giving Him adoration and thanksgiving, the veil is rent and His glory pours out to flood the soul and body.

The exercises and means of preparation we looked at in the previous chapter, all work to help dissolve the remnants of the veil between spirit and soul. As the glory of God flows out of the Holy of Holies, we are changed in profound ways and God is able to make Himself known to others through us. We are His individual temples and He desires to fill us with His glory to overflowing.

As we serve the Lord in the temple of our own lives, He is then able to place us as living stones as He builds the corporate temple that will be the dwelling place for His glory, before all things have been completed in the earth.

When the glory is released through a purified vessel, it dramatically impacts whatever it touches. Creative miracles, healing, translation in the spirit, open visions, suspending the laws of physics to do things like walk on water, and walk through walls are all effortless when the glory of God is released through His saints. These things will become more common as we come closer to the end of this age. God will have a witness in the earth like no other time in history in the last days. Jesus said that those who believe in Him would do the works He did and even greater things.[122] The church hasn't even come close to fulfilling this yet. So, you can count on quite a spectacular display of His glory in the days ahead.

---

[122] Jn 14:12

Does this mean that every Christian will walk in signs and wonders and manifest miracles of immense power? Will every person who names Christ as Lord carry the glory of God to the nations in the days to come? The answer will be discovered as we study various aspects of the vessel of God's glory seen in the Old Testament – the ark of the covenant.

**Activation**

*Lord, I ask You to shape and fit me as a living stone in Your holy temple. Draw me into the holy of holies, where I might see Your glory and minister before You in awe and adoration. Please take me through the processes of cleansing, sacrifice, and intimacy with Your Spirit, and please feed and sustain me as I draw near to You. Thank You, Lord of Glory for showing me the way. Amen.*

## Chapter 13
§

# The Ark

Within the most holy place of the temple of God was the ark of the testimony. The glory of God would rest upon the ark and was seen by the priest when he came to minister before the Lord once a year.

The ark was the chosen vessel that God's glory would come to rest upon. It is a type of the human vessels that will carry the glory of God and the testimony of Jesus in a way that is beyond our imagination, at the time of this book's writing. Let's consider the construction and design of the ark to get a better idea of what the end-time servants of God, that will have the glory rest upon them in a remarkable way, will be like.

The ark was constructed of acacia wood, which is resistant to decay. The core material was cut from trees, which speaks of natural man. The wood was covered with pure gold, representing the purification by fire laid over the inner man. The incorruptible gold serves to protect and preserve the wooden core.

The chosen vessels that will carry the glory of God to the nations in the final hours of this age will be refined by fire and have a core inner strength that is resistant to corruption. Having separated themselves unto God, they will not be given to the things of this world. They will have submitted to the fiery trials and dealings of God, being emptied of anything that would lead them into judgment.

Desire for anything but the glory of God will have no place in them. This is the gold that protects them from the temptations and pressures to be drawn away from the focused extreme mission that the Lord commissions them to. Wealth, comfort, the lusts of the flesh, desire for recognition, the fear of man, and the fear of suffering will hold no sway with them, as they have become resistant to corruption and compromise. They will seek the pleasure of the Lord, rather than their own.

The top of the ark had two cherubim, crafted of gold, facing each other with their wings outstretched, one toward the other. This was called the mercy seat and is where the glory would come to rest. This represents the high level angelic assignments over the lives of those that the glory will rest upon.

The cherubim are a high ranking order of angel that will serve in ministry to God as well as those the Lord clothes with His glory. Jesus is our High Priest, the Intercessor and the Mediator of the better covenant we enjoy in Him. He is the qualification and the qualifier for our relationship with God. So, these angels do not qualify one for the glory, but are assigned to minister to God's chosen vessels. They help in the process of preparation and open the heavens to make way for the glory of God to rest upon these servants of the Lord.

Inside the ark were the stone tablets that Moses brought down from the mountain of God inscribed with the testimony, or Law, given to the people from the Lord, a golden bowl containing some of the manna that the Lord sustained Israel with in the wilderness, and Aaron's rod that bloomed in the desert[123]. Each of these things is a type of what will be found within the elect servants of God in the last days. In the next chapter we will look at some of the specific things that these bondservants of the Lord will do and see their place in the dramatic climax of this age. An introduction to their characteristics here will help to build a foundation for chapter fourteen.

The forerunners that will have the glory of God rest upon them will carry the testimony of God. Just as Moses was a prophet that delivered the mandates of the Lord to the people, these saints will proclaim and prophesy the end-time purposes of God to the church and to the nations. They will deliver the mandates of God in preparing the way for the Lord's coming, much like John the Baptist. They will be witnesses of the glory and majesty of Jesus

---

[123] Heb 9:2-5

and proclaim His Lordship over all things. As prophets, like none that have gone before them, they will bring glory to Jesus and testify of His nature and character, proclaiming Him to be Lord, Bridegroom, King of Kings, Judge, Savior, the Son of God.[124]

The urn of manna represents the miraculous provision of God in sustaining these servants, both physically and spiritually. Manna from heaven will be their source of life, comfort and strength. They will carry high levels of revelation as they are fed from the hand of God. They will give out of the true bread they carry to bring others into a deeper knowledge of the Lord.

The rod that budded in the desert represents God given authority and a ministry marked by signs and wonders. The staff of authority they carry will appear to be a simple stick to some. Wrapped in an unassuming, humble and natural looking package will be the authority to perform great works of healing and miracles, as many Christians will do.

But the carriers of glory will also release unusually powerful signs and wonders. The very judgments of God will be released by them. Their words will be empowered to pierce the hearts of people with the conviction, love, mercy and judgments of God. The bloom represents the beauty and life that will spring forth from these instruments of God's authority in the earth. They will make known the beauty and majesty of the Lord.

There are some who are called to walk a radically set apart life unto God. The Lord will not allow them to participate in and enjoy certain things that are allowed for others. Their primary calling is to minister to the Lord in the secret place. They will be misunderstood and wrongly judged. The closer they come to Jesus and the further from the world, the more they will be rejected, even by many in the church. Others will call them "hyper-spiritual," unbalanced and even lazy. God will not allow them to be slandered forever, and will set them apart among their brethren after the season of their preparation is complete.

The glory of God will rest on those among them chosen as His end-time arks. They will be used mightily in releasing the works of the Lord in the days to come. Not all forerunners will be carriers of

---

[124] Rev 19:10

the glory in this way, but all of the end-time arks of the Lord will be forerunners. Some forerunners will be used for various other unusual and noble purposes. God's sovereign choice and the level of preparation obtained by each person called as a forerunner will determine the nature of their particular functions.

Many are called but few are chosen,[125] even among forerunners. Many will drop out of the intense boot camp and training program the Lord puts them through and forfeit the fullness of their calling. God has engineered their circumstances and lives to keep them in the crucible of His dealings, while others are celebrating and enjoying the good things God has blessed them with (not that this is wrong). The reward of the forerunner is found in God alone.

The true forerunners of God won't walk in pride, at least not for long. If you aren't called to this you don't want to try to be one of these folks. They pay an extreme price and God holds them to a stricter standard than others. The pressures upon them from the forces of darkness, the intense trials and tests of God, and the pain of not fitting into the "normal" structure of society and the church are beyond what others can imagine. It requires a particular fortitude and humility that is made available to them by way of the Lord's peculiar grace for them.

I'm sure some will disagree with my assertion that only a select group of people are called to a purpose unlike the majority of Christians. While I don't care much for the elitism that is in the church these days in other regards, the Lord has impressed this upon me and it seems clear to me that Scripture also supports this notion. All saints are called to prepare for the glory of the Lord and enter into it before His wonderful appearing, but relatively few will actually be carriers of the glory. We will examine further evidence of this as we go along.

The pattern of God choosing a select few to walk in differing levels of glory and authority is seen throughout the Bible. Two particular witnesses to this parallel each other, in many ways.

---

[125] Mt 22:1-14

## Realms of Glory ☼ 13 – The Ark

In the days of Moses there were the multitudes, the seventy elders, the twelve chiefs, and the three appointed priests, and among those there was one chosen above the others; that is Aaron.[126]

Jesus was the prophet to come like Moses,[127] and we see the same pattern in the ministry of Jesus. There were the multitudes, the seventy-two He sent out with a level of authority to preach the message of the Kingdom[128], the twelve apostles, three of which He took with Him to the Mount of Transfiguration, and the one – John the Beloved, who received the Revelation of Jesus Christ and was the only of the twelve to die of old age.

In Numbers chapter 16 is recorded the rebellion of Korah. We can learn much from this tragic episode of God's chosen leaders being challenged. Korah, along with 250 others, claimed to be equal in function and position with Moses and Aaron because the Lord was among the people. They dishonored God by rejecting His sovereign order of leadership. The lost lives of their families, as well as their own, were the penalty paid for this rebellion.

Even though the people of Israel saw the severity of God's judgment on these rebels, they continued to murmur against Moses and Aaron. God struck down 14,700 of them with plague before Moses could stop the judgment of God in intercession.

In chapter 17 of Numbers, in His mercy, God again gives the people a sign of who carried true authority to lead the people. Aaron and all the chiefs gave their staffs to Moses, who placed the staffs in the tent of meeting. The next day Aaron's rod had bloomed, while the others had not. God then commanded that Aaron's staff be placed in the ark of the testimony as a sign to the rebels.[129]

We are entering a time when the judgments of God against rebels will become as severe as we have seen here. When God manifests His glory and marks vessels by His sovereign will to carry the glory or to lead people, it is a direct affront to the Lord to challenge or deny His sovereign choice.

---

[126] Ex 24:1-2, Num 1:44-45, Num 17:10-11
[127] Dt 18:15-18
[128] Lk 10:1
[129] Num 17:10-11

It is common for people to covet the gifts and callings of another. We must guard against such error if we are to finish well before the Lord. Some exceptionally anointed ministers of the Lord did not complete their race or fell into sin because they stepped outside the boundaries of their God given authority, gifting or calling. There are clear warnings throughout the Bible about coveting and usurping the rightful authority given to another, from Genesis to Revelation.

*Jude 6-8*
*And the angels **who did not stay within their own position of authority, but left their proper dwelling**, he has kept in eternal chains under gloomy darkness until the judgment of the great day — just as Sodom and Gomorrah and the surrounding cities, which likewise indulged in sexual immorality and pursued unnatural desire, serve as an example by undergoing a punishment of eternal fire. **Yet in like manner these people** also, relying on their dreams, defile the flesh, **reject authority**, and blaspheme the glorious ones.*

We all have limits and boundaries that we must operate within to maintain our authority and stay within God's will. The same attitude of dishonor seen in the rebellion of Korah and warned about by Jude, that denies God ordains some to walk in higher levels of anointing, glory, authority, and gifting, has risen in the church.

It seems that when we err in the church we tend to over-correct toward the opposite extreme. Many have been wounded by leadership in the church, but this does not justify a reaction that leads to rebellion against God's order for leadership. In reaction to false authority taken outside of its divinely set limits, some rebel or claim an egalitarian view in all respects is God's order. We are all equal in value and equally eligible to have access to intimate relationship with God.

Yet, we are not all equal in function, anointing, authority, and position. God did not make us homogenous. He has designed us to fulfill specific functions and roles, according to His sovereign will.

Failure to recognize this and come into agreement with God's order of things will present major problems for many in the days ahead.

If we aren't claiming that all people are equal in authority and function, then it seems we are trying to claim position and authority that does not belong to us. To err in either direction is to open the door to witchcraft. Both rebellion and control are the roots of witchcraft, which is to tear down God's order of authority and give control to the powers of darkness.

The ascension gift ministries are given to the church as gifts to help equip the saints to fulfill *their* (the saint's) ministry.[130] "Fivefold" ministers are servants to help train and mentor those who will go into the world to expand the Kingdom. An authoritarian approach to leadership, and the pride, manipulative, controlling and domineering tactics, used by some holding leadership positions in the church, are not the Lord's way of leading people. It is witchcraft, and should not be tolerated in the church. Our distorted view of authority will soon be corrected. The message of Ezekiel chapter 34 would be a good thing for all of us to carefully consider.

Authority in the spirit realm does not always equate with authority to lead people. High levels of anointing and gifting are not always the marks of one called to a specific ministry function or to leadership.

So, as I discussed in chapter eleven, lack of title and position should not present a barrier to fulfilling one's call. Ordination by man only has value within the structures of man. In most cases, it has nothing to do with God's Kingdom or the ability to fulfill one's role under His rule. This has not been understood because most are looking within the structure of the church as the place for their ministry and calling. In reality, the vast majority of believers are called to ministry in the world, outside of the organized church.

The current trend in the church to claim apostleship without the accompanying signs of an apostle will put those who make such claims in great danger as the true apostles of Christ are revealed. The Lord is patient and has overlooked this kind of immaturity, as much of it has come out of ignorance, rather than rebellion.

---

[130] Eph 4:11-16

However, when the power and authority of the true apostolic arrives, those who would challenge God's appointed leaders, or assert their own authority outside the limits of what God has set, will place themselves in great peril. The army described in Joel chapter 2 is a picture of these fearsome warriors of the Lord.

Reformation is coming, but not in the way that most have imagined. We must not let our preconceived notions about what the church will look like hinder the work of God in implementing what He desires. He is not giving the blueprints to anyone, as we would just build something askew of His perfect will out of our limited understanding.

All Christians are called to do the works that Jesus did and walk in the supernatural. God desires for all of us to come to know Him in deep intimate union. We can all prepare to explore the realms of heaven and the glory.

But we are not all called to carry the glory. Not all are called to lead. We are all given the same Spirit, but He decides how He will manifest through each person. This does not make one superior or more acceptable to the Lord, just different in function.[131]

Your eternal reward in the glory is not determined by your anointing, gifting or calling on earth. You will be rewarded based on your level of obedience and stewardship in what God gives you, not by what He ordains for someone else. Become all that you can be using what God has gifted you with to accomplish His will for your life while relying on Him to be your strength, in humility, and your reward will be great.

So, what is the proper way to view these unusual servants of God and how should we respond to them? How do we prepare for the glory of the Lord as a corporate Body of believers? Let's consider some of the other biblical accounts concerning the ark to see what we can learn about all of this.

The ark went before Israel through the desert and ahead of them into battle. The glory of the Lord made way before the congregation and the warriors to break open new territory and take ground. The spoils of war and possession of the promises came as a direct result

---

[131] Paul addressed this issue in *1 Cor 12:12-31*.

of the proper handling and positioning of the ark. There are many stories in the Old Testament depicting this.

The ark went ahead of the people by three days. This is a picture of the forerunner going ahead to prepare the way of the Lord. Elijah and John the Baptist are examples of God's radically consecrated forerunners. They were completely set apart and committed to the purposes of God, without regard for personal sacrifice or the approval of anyone, save God.

So will it be in the days ahead, as forerunners carry the glory ahead of the people of God to break open new spiritual territory. The bounty of what is gained there will be made available to all of the Lord's servants, regardless of role or function. The heavens will be opened by them and the realms of glory made accessible by these end-time "arks" of God.

The Lord revealed to Moses His will for transporting the ark before Israel. The ark was carried by seven priests from the tribe of Levi.[132] This was one of the requirements for the people to enter the land of promise.[133] Even though a select few would carry the ark of the Lord and lead the way, all of the people of God, who obeyed Him, would enter into the land and enjoy its bounty. All of the people were able to see the glory of God and benefit from it, but not all carried it.

In 2 Samuel 6, and in the parallel account in 1 Chronicles 13, is the story of the ark being brought to Jerusalem by David. There are some interesting things that can be seen here concerning God's order for the right handling of the ark and the consequences of ignoring them.

The first thing to note is that David consulted with the leaders of Israel, rather than God and the Scriptures, regarding the transportation of the ark. This was the first mistake made by the leaders of Israel. Though the desire to have the ark and the glory resident with them was noble and good, the way in which they approached appropriating it was contrary to God's order.

Today there are many leaders who are consulting with each other about how to get the glory into the church. God will not bless

---

[132] Deut 10:8
[133] Deut 10:11

the programs, plans and ways of man. He will not have the handling of His glory come under the direction of leadership. Again, we see that a call to leadership does not mean one is qualified to carry the glory. Seeking for the habitation of God within our assemblies is good, but we must seek for His glory to come in strict accordance with His requirements.

The ark was located on a hill in Gibeah. It is thought by some scholars that this was the hill called Gibeah of Saul; the place where King Saul was born. Saul started out well with a heart turned toward the Lord, but was ultimately rejected by God because he did not do things according to God's instructions. Saul stepped outside of God's zone of authority given to the king and assumed the role of God's priest, by making a sacrifice to the Lord.[134]

King Saul operated outside of God's order and timing. This became a pattern in Saul's life that cost him everything. Later, Saul also disobeyed by not utterly destroying the Amalekites and all of their goods and livestock.[135] Saul is the consummate example of what neglect and rebellion lead to. Witchcraft, murder and suicide were the result of Saul's disobedience.

Again we see a picture of the desires of leaders being toward the Lord, but in their impatience and out of neglect to obey His commands they get into serious trouble. Desiring the glory is good, but pursuing it apart from the timing and specific direction of the Lord will lead to disaster.

At that time, the ark was kept in the house of Abinadab, and remained there for over twenty years. The name Abinadab can be translated to mean either *"father is noble," "my father is willing"* or *"father of willingness,"* or *"father of liberality."* This shows that Father God, the keeper of glory and the ark that it rests on, is noble and willing to liberally pour out His glory and have it come to fill His temple; the people of God.

So, we should understand that God was willing for the ark to go and be among the people. He is liberal in showing His glory to those who approach it with the proper reverence and according to His ways.

---

[134] 1 Sam 13:8-15
[135] 1 Sam 15

The next misstep made was that the ark was placed on a new cart drawn by oxen. The new cart is the vehicle of man that was devised after the leadership council decided how to get the ark to Jerusalem. God's explicit instructions in Scripture were that the ark be carried by men of the priesthood.

The new cart is the new program, method, structure or other contrivance of man that is built in presumption. God will not let His glory rest on the initiatives, agendas or structures of man, no matter how noble the motivation. The over-emphasis of the "new wineskin" teaching on the "five-fold" ministry being the container that God will fill with His glory, as discussed in chapter eleven, is a modern day example of this.

While God does anoint and appoint apostles, prophets, evangelists, pastors and teachers in the church, this does not automatically qualify these leaders to carry the glory. Likewise a chosen vessel of the Lord who will carry the glory is not necessarily called to a place of leadership in the church. Some will be anointed to be both. In any case, we must make room for and honor one another as the Lord sees fit to use us for His pleasure.

The new cart also depicts leadership's failure to recognize the ark as the chosen vessel of God. This is similar to the cookie-cutter programs we design to "disciple" people. Forerunners don't fit into the mould created by our religious systems. To insist that they just be carried along by a program that is not tailored to their individual callings and then expect to see them mature into what God has ordained for them is to neglect the specific will of God for each one's path in the Kingdom.

The oxen used to draw the cart shows further contempt for the ark as natural beasts are used to move it along. This indicates the lack of willingness to make the proper effort and sacrifice to see the chosen vessels of God come into the place He has prepared for them. It takes work and humility for leaders to support and carry along forerunners to see them come into the fullness of their callings. Expecting the glory to fill the church while disrespecting or neglecting God's anointed carriers of the glory is an insult to Him and will exact a heavy penalty.

Next we see that the ark came to the threshing floor of Nacon. Nacon means *"of a certainty," "to a set place," "firm,"* or *"prepared."* It is a certainty that the carriers of God's glory will come to the threshing floor to be *prepared* and made *firm* for the immense challenges they will face. Chapters eight, nine, ten and eleven of this book deal with this extensively.

It is also a certainty that the cart will be upset when it comes to the set place of the threshing floor. God is going to shake loose all that has not been commissioned by His Spirit. Some tables and carts are about to get turned over in the house of God.

The oxen stumble here and the cart tips, placing the ark in jeopardy. As Uzzah, who was helping his brother Ahio drive the cart, reaches out to steady the ark and prevent it from falling, the anger of the Lord breaks out against him and Uzzah is killed. The name Uzzah means strength.[136]

Anyone who reaches out for the glory in their own strength and presumes that they are able to uphold it, protect it, or otherwise handle it, put themselves at extreme risk of being dealt with by the Lord in a severe manner. This also illustrates the warning God gives us regarding the mistreatment of His chosen vessels.[137]

The ark was then taken to the house of Obed-Edom, as fear and anger came upon David over the incident of Uzzah's death. Obed-Edom was a Levite. The ark stayed in his home for several months and Obed-Edom, along with his entire family, were blessed and prospered during that time.

Obed-Edom can mean *"servant of God," "servant of man,"* or *"servant of the earth."* I see Obed-Edom as being a servant of the Lord (Levite), a servant of man and of the earth. He desires to please God by serving his fellow man and tend the earth, according to God's commands.

There are many people who have been shunned by the church or have been turned-off to organized religion because the power of God is seldom seen in the church. The absence of the glory and our failure to demonstrate what the Word promises, speaks louder than our carefully crafted sermons and empty programs. Today's church can't keep the interest of those who are looking for something real.

---

[136] The name Uzzah means strength, just as the name Uzziah also means strength. We looked at how this relates to the glory in chapter nine of this book when we considered Isaiah's encounter with God in the glory, as recorded in Isa. 6.
[137] 1 Chron 16:19-22

Obed-Edom wants God, but he can live without the politics, window dressing and flashy programs.

Understand that I like a well crafted sermon and a cohesive message. I also enjoy a good laugh along the way through a timely message from the Lord. Effective communication and precise targeting are essential in delivering a message with power. I also think that we should use every means at our disposal, in media and technology, to preach the gospel and deliver a precise and relatable message to the world. Humor, personal stories and media can be skillfully used as spice to add flavor to a message.

However, just as with food, too much spice will make an otherwise wholesome meal inedible. Sadly, jokes, stories and anecdotes are often overused to cover a message that lacks any real meat. Too often these days, the power of a direct and anointed delivery of God's Word is sacrificed for "relevance," and illustrations drawn from contemporary culture.

The Joshua generation that is coming forth won't need clever, mind-numbing sermon illustrations and cute stories to make their message palatable. Their words will be empowered beyond anything heard throughout history. Their very lives will be the message and the sermon illustration.

We are about to have our level of love and humility tested, as God harvests forerunners out of the world and quickly matures them. These young firebrands will grow in the knowledge and fear of the Lord and will be released into powerful ministries in short order. The level of anointing, gifting, character and revelation they walk in will be beyond what we have ever seen. We must guard against jealousy. We need to nurture, support and make a place for God's end-time arks of glory.

Obed-Edom is a picture of those who pursue God in humility and gladly welcome His agents of the glory. They will take the forerunners of God in and give them safe haven and shelter. God will bless these servants of man who gladly welcome His glory in whatever package the Lord chooses. Their hearts will be to support and bless the servants of God who will carry the glory to the world and make Him known.

The message and ministry of the forerunner will be rejected by many in the church initially. God will then bring them outside the organized church and send them to those in the world who are hungry for the glory of God. Like Obed-Edom, they will be humble and receive these carriers of the glory with joy and thanksgiving. They will make place for the forerunners and take them in, giving them support and meeting their practical needs.

The forerunners will teach and mentor them in the ways of the Spirit and bring them into intimate relationship with the Lord of Glory. Like Obed-Edom, they will be blessed and prosper ahead of many in the church who fail to receive the servants of God and give them support.

David became angry over the death of Uzzah. So will some leaders in the church become upset when the programs and plans they have devised fail to bring the glory into their assemblies. God will lay waste to the structures that come out of man's strength. The fire that comes just ahead of the cloud of glory will consume everything not born of the Spirit.

When the carriers of glory emerge their very presence will reveal the impure motives in those who desire to have their name associated with this mighty move of God. Many ministers now expect that they will be the ones to usher in the next outpouring of the glory. Some will reject the forerunners, and therefore the glory, in jealousy and pride. It will be offensive to them to see the glory of God rest on simple unassuming servants who they deem unqualified, rather than on themselves.

Like David who was provoked to jealousy when he heard of the great blessing that was upon the house of Obed-Edom, so will some leaders in the church desire to bring the ark of God into the tabernacle by seeking God for His will and instructions. Once they see that the glory continues to rest upon His servants, and that those outside their camp are being favored for receiving them, some will repent and seek to have the ark of glory come into their fellowships. Their motives will be purified and they will humbly receive the chosen vessels of God with the proper respect and humility.

Support has been withheld in many ways from God's emerging new forerunners. The Body of Christ will be called upon to support these servants of the Lord financially, in intercession, and in other practical areas to facilitate their ministry to the Lord, the church and the world. Even as some are called to minister before the Lord in continual fasting and prayer, like at the International House of Prayer in Kansas City, financial support will be required to facilitate their ministry and training.

God is raising up end-time ministers of finance who have the anointing of Joseph the patriarch. Some will be used to finance the ministries of forerunners. But many in the church will fail to see the hand of God upon the end-time vessels of glory and withhold support.

Yet God will provide. "The gold is in the fish's mouth," the Lord once said to me. I understand this to mean that there are wealthy people in the world right now who will be touched by the power and glory of God carried by His forerunners. These fish, now waiting to be harvested, will have ferocious devotion to God as they come into contact with something more real and satisfying than anything that religion has to offer. In gratitude, and as directed by the Lord, they will make provision for God's arks of glory to fulfill their ministries.

Those who reject and withhold from these special ministers of God's glory will miss the reward He desires to give them. Some will have what has been entrusted to them taken away for failing to steward according to God's commands.

We must get over our traditional mindsets of what "ministry" is and be willing to get behind those who are called to walk a path radically different from what we have seen up to this point. Some of these chosen vessels will remain relatively hidden and operate "underground." They will be able to move in and out of nations quickly on precise covert operations that larger well known ministries could not safely manage during times of upheaval. Their intense training will prepare them to go into dangerous situations and effect dramatic change undetected, in the natural and spirit realms. These sold-out special operations soldiers of Christ are no less deserving of aid and support than a traditional 501C3 (non-profit) organization.

An army that withholds the basic needs of its soldiers, especially its special forces, is doomed to defeat. God will meet the needs of His end-time warriors one way or another. His first choice would be for those He calls to support His forerunners to share in the victory and bounty of what is taken in battle by them.

So, as the vessels of glory chosen by God begin to surface and are revealed, we must be ready to receive and support them. In so doing the glory of the Lord will be brought into His household and will abide with us. This will test the humility, love, and devotion of many, as these radical servants of God will not fit into the paradigm of what many expect.

Just as Jesus was offensive to the religious leaders in the first century and as He exposed the evil condition of their hearts, so will these forerunners cause a stir among those in the church who are self-seeking. And just as was true with Jesus, the humble and simple will receive them and their ministry as God's glory is revealed through them.

When David brought the ark up out of the house of Obed-Edom, he gave instructions for the proper carrying of the ark. Every six steps along the way to Jerusalem an ox and a fattened animal were sacrificed. The ox is a beast of burden and work. Six is the number of man. The seventh step represents the Sabbath rest. Jesus is now the Sabbath rest for all who are in Him.[138]

So, we see that human strength, labor and burdens were given up as a sacrifice in recognition of God's perfect rest and completed work in Christ. We must acknowledge in thought, word and deed that Christ in us is the only thing that qualifies us to enter into the glory. The sacrifice of all human effort and initiative must be made regularly if we are to have the glory dwell among us. The work of the Lord comes out of our place of rest in Him. We must continually acknowledge Him as the source and ascribe all glory to Him, lest we touch His glory.

One of the mandates that I was given by the Lord during the week long visitation described in chapter seven was, *"to help train up Joel's army."* The Lord told me to *"Give My young forerunners sanctuary and a place to grow in the things of the Spirit."*

My wife and I have received numerous prophetic words over the years concerning this as well. A vision of a large house on some acreage where young prophetic eagles would come to be nurtured and protected in preparation for their end-time missions, has been a common image seen by others over us, and in Patti's dreams. It will

---

[138] Heb 4:9-11

be a place of refuge during perilous times for a few of God's young warriors.

This will be one of many places that the Lord establishes to mentor and take care of the practical needs of His arks of glory. We aren't taking applications, and will not be recruiting to get anyone into the "program." The Lord will bring the few that He selects to us. I mention it only to introduce the idea, and as confirmation to others who have sensed similar things. God is raising up these places of refuge for young eagles.

The Lord is now speaking to more people about establishing or helping to support similar works. This doesn't fit inside the nicely packaged programs and structure of the organized church, and neither do the extreme firebrands of God that are emerging.

Some are studying the revivalists of past moves of God and trying to analyze what they did to get God to move now. This is futile. It is a veiled attempt to get God to meet us on our terms. The thinking is that if we can do what they did then, God will do what He did then, for us now.

Studying the men and women of God who have been effective, and past revivals, is useful in understanding where there may be keys to unlock the wells of revival in our time. However, God is not a machine or a computer that we can go to and punch in the right sequence of codes and then expect Him to dispense what we are after. To approach God in this manner is to neglect His person and lightly esteem His desire for relationship and interaction. God is immutable (His nature never changes), but He is always doing new things. The promises He gives us are contingent on obedience to the specific commands He gives in a given situation.

God wants us to quit looking to the past to find the future. While there is value in studying the revivals of the past, history, and the Bible to gain understanding of certain principles and come to grasp prophetic revelation that is now being released, we must not build according to the patterns of the past, apart from the clear direction and timing of the Lord. We have not been this way before. We will miss it if we don't listen, obey and flow in what He is doing now in preparation for what He will be doing next.

What the great revivalists of the past did was allow God to empty them of self and presumption. They didn't develop big plans and strategies. They developed an intimate friendship with Him and were changed by continually gazing upon His glory. Then they walked in union and obedience to Him in the moment, just as Jesus did. That's it - no formula.

I do not mean that God never gives prophetic plans and strategies for building what He desires, even many years in advance. To build anything of significance will take planning and strategizing. But we must not develop our plans and build according to our own understanding or the patterns of the past, apart from clear inspiration and instruction from the Lord. A continual posture of waiting and yielding must be maintained throughout the process to keep things on track. God often redirects or diverts our efforts as we go along.

God will not be packaged, analyzed, coerced, or made to fill the structures of man's making. He desires eternal relationship. So many just want to have the power, anointing, gifting, ministry, work, glory, fame, money, experiences, knowledge and wisdom and don't really want Him. God cannot be studied and used. He must be pursued, known and adored.

God is doing a new thing in the Body of Christ and in the earth. We must lay aside our expectations and presumptions about what this all means so that we do not run counter to God's purposes. One thing is certain; God has many surprises in store for us.

What is this all leading up to then? Has God given us any clues at all about what is ahead? Certainly He makes known what He is doing, in the proper time. With the understanding gained from what we have covered up to this point, we can now catch a glimpse of what is in store for us in that day.

**Activation**

*Father, I ask You to help me to understand my place in Your Kingdom. Lord, teach me the deeper truths concerning authority, leadership and submission. Show me the areas in my heart and mind where I may be holding ungodly beliefs that are contrary to Your divine order of government. Lord, open my thinking and help me to hear and understand Your specific strategies and instructions for me in fulfilling my part in Your end-time purposes. Help me to trust in You with all of my heart, rather than using my own limited understanding and abilities to accomplish Your will. Thank You for Your great love, grace and for the glory You are releasing to me in greater measure. Praise the name of the Lord Jesus forever!*

# Chapter 14
§

# In That Day

Before Christ returns to establish His earthly reign, the knowledge of the glory of the Lord will be made known throughout the earth. God will reveal His nature and character in the release of His glory, in unprecedented measure and quality.

*Hab 2:14*
*For the earth will be filled*
*with the knowledge of the glory of the LORD*
*as the waters cover the sea.*

Many like to quote this verse from the book of Habakkuk with excited anticipation of the great blessing that will be poured out when the glory comes.

However, this verse is sandwiched in between some rather disturbing warnings and prophetic declarations concerning the time of this outpouring. If we read this verse within its immediate context, an altogether different picture begins to develop.

*Hab 2:2-20*
*And the LORD answered me: "Write the vision; make it plain on tablets, so he may run who reads it. For still the vision awaits its appointed time; it hastens to the end — it will not lie. If it seems slow, wait for it; it will surely come; it will not delay. "Behold, his soul is puffed up; it is not upright within him, but the righteous shall live by his faith.*
*"Moreover, wine is a traitor, an arrogant man who is never at rest. His greed is as wide as Sheol; like death he has never enough. He gathers for himself all nations and collects*

as his own all peoples." Shall not all these take up their taunt against him, with scoffing and riddles for him, and say, "Woe to him who heaps up what is not his own — for how long? — and loads himself with pledges!" Will not your debtors suddenly arise, and those awake who will make you tremble? Then you will be spoil for them. Because you have plundered many nations, all the remnant of the peoples shall plunder you, for the blood of man and violence to the earth, to cities and all who dwell in them. "Woe to him who gets evil gain for his house, to set his nest on high, to be safe from the reach of harm! You have devised shame for your house by cutting off many peoples; you have forfeited your life. For the stone will cry out from the wall, and the beam from the woodwork respond. "Woe to him who builds a town with blood and founds a city on iniquity! Behold, is it not from the LORD of hosts that peoples labor merely for fire, and nations weary themselves for nothing? **For the earth will be filled with the knowledge of the glory of the LORD as the waters cover the sea.** "Woe to him who makes his neighbors drink — you pour out your wrath and make them drunk, in order to gaze at their nakedness! **You will have your fill of shame instead of glory.** Drink, yourself, and show your uncircumcision! The cup in the LORD's right hand will come around to you, and utter shame will come upon your glory! The violence done to Lebanon will overwhelm you, as will the destruction of the beasts that terrified them, for the blood of man and violence to the earth, to cities and all who dwell in them. "What profit is an idol when its maker has shaped it, a metal image, a teacher of lies? For its maker trusts in his own creation when he makes speechless idols! Woe to him who says to a wooden thing, Awake; to a silent stone, Arise! Can this teach? Behold, it is overlaid with gold and silver, and there is no breath at all in it. **But the LORD is in his holy temple**; let all the earth keep silence before him."

God's glory will be seen in His Holy Temple; the purified saints. For many others there will be great woe, wrath and shame.

We must not ignore these strong words because they don't make us comfortable or fit our current paradigm. Far too much is written in the Bible concerning the immense level of spiritual blessing, and the judgments of God that will be released in that day, for us to treat these warnings casually.

The effects of this revelation of God's character, through the outpouring of His glory, will vary depending on each individual's heart condition and level of preparation. To those who have prepared themselves, in the ways we have considered throughout this book, great blessing and the fulfillment of God's promises to His saints will be released in ways and degrees beyond our current understanding.

However, to those who neglect the fear of the Lord in failing to respond and prepare, fearful judgment will be the experienced effect of the manifest glory. Both great blessing and severe judgment will be poured out beyond anything yet imagined, in the great and terrible Day of the Lord. We can see this illustrated and foretold throughout both Testaments of Scripture. Isaiah 60 is a classic example of this.

In Luke 4:19 Jesus quoted the prophet Isaiah from chapter 61 verses 1 and 2. The Lord was proclaiming Himself to be the Messiah written of by Isaiah. The full two verses He quoted from read:

> *Isa 61:1-2*
> *The Spirit of the Lord GOD is upon me,*
> *because the LORD has anointed me*
> *to bring good news to the poor;*
> *he has sent me to bind up the brokenhearted,*
> *to proclaim liberty to the captives,*
> *and the opening of the prison to those who are bound;*
> *to proclaim the year of the LORD's favor,*
> *and the day of vengeance of our God;*
> *to comfort all who mourn;*

The Lord stopped short in verse 2 with *"to proclaim the year of the LORD's favor"*. He did not proclaim *"the day of vengeance of our God; to comfort all who mourn"* at that time. The time of

God's favor upon all mankind is symbolically called a *year,* while the time of His vengeance is comparatively short, being called a *day.* Mercy triumphs over judgment.[139] So, we can be grateful the satisfaction of His wrath will be completed over a short period of time.

We are now living out the last portion of the *year of the Lord's favor* and about to enter into the time of *the day of His vengeance.* This does not mean that His mercy will be withdrawn altogether, but it is a time when His judgments will be released in an effort to draw all who will come into His Kingdom to do so. People will be "sealed" into their destinies during this time.[140]

Threaded throughout the Minor Prophets we see the same theme as well. The book of Joel is especially focused on the Day of the Lord, and the outpouring of God's Spirit, glory and wrath at the end of the age.

> *Joel 2:1-2*
> *Let all the inhabitants of the land tremble,*
> *for the day of the LORD is coming; it is near,*
> *a day of darkness and gloom,*
> ***a day of clouds and thick darkness!***

We will see the thick clouds of the Lord's glory cover the earth. In conjunction with this unparalleled outpouring of God's glory, will be the release of His judgments, on those who have shunned His mercy. To some it will bring the joy and pleasure of having their deepest longings satisfied, and to others it will mean their destruction.

> *Joel 3:18-21*
> *"And **in that day**
> *the mountains shall drip sweet wine,*
> *and the hills shall flow with milk,*
> *and all the streambeds of Judah*
> *shall flow with water;*

---

[139] James 2:13
[140] Rev 7:3-4, 9:4, 13:16, 14:9, 17:5

*and a fountain shall come forth from the house of the LORD
and water the Valley of Shittim.*

*"Egypt shall become a desolation
and Edom a desolate wilderness,
for the violence done to the people of Judah,
because they have shed innocent blood in their land.
But Judah shall be inhabited forever,
and Jerusalem to all generations.
I will avenge their blood,
blood I have not avenged,
for the LORD dwells in Zion."*

Understanding the nature of the times that we are entering into is of vital importance, even as the ways of preparation we have already considered are. Many people are under the delusion that they will not have to endure through the time of Great Tribulation at the end of this age. While times are going to be tough in many respects, God has made provision for us to flourish, in His Spirit, in the midst of great trouble.

I believe that the great apostasy, or falling away[141], will be comprised largely of folks who are disillusioned and totally unprepared when things start to get tough, because they have misunderstood the nature of His appearing and the means of preparation required to endure. Besides having to face some nasty circumstances unprepared, those who aren't ready will miss out on the best action a Christian could hope for. That's when we'll see the glory manifest like no other time in history. We all have the opportunity to be right in the middle of the wonder and drama that are now unfolding.[142] You don't want to miss this show!

God is about to visit His temple and fill it with His glory like never before.[143] This is your shelter and your refuge. It is the place of peace in the midst of great unrest; the place where the glory dwells.

---

[141] Mt 24:10-13, 2 Thes 2:3
[142] 2 Thes 1:5-11
[143] Hag 2:6-9

I will limit this presentation to aspects of eschatology (the study of last things, or the last days) that relate directly to the outpouring of glory that is coming, as it was introduced earlier in this chapter. I hope to write more extensively on these topics in the future, should the Lord desire it. So, a few salient points here, and my recommendation that you study these things for yourself, will have to suffice for now.

Psalm 91 will be the anthem of those who learn to live in the realms of glory, while walking through dark times. The steadfast faith of those great men and women in the Bible, who saw the salvation of God in impossible circumstances, will become an integral part of our existence, as we learn to abide in the glory. The glory realm will serve as a protective shield for us as we come into increasingly perilous times.

> *Ps 3:3*
> *But you, O LORD, are a shield about me,*
> *my glory, and the lifter of my head.*

The book of Revelation foretells some of the spectacular events that are now on the horizon. The forerunners and vessels of God's glory mentioned in chapter 13 of this book are seen in several places in John's visions.

> *Rev 7:2-4*
> *Then I saw another angel ascending from the rising of the sun, with the seal of the living God, and he called with a loud voice to the four angels who had been given power to harm earth and sea, saying, "Do not harm the earth or the sea or the trees, until we have sealed the servants of our God on their foreheads." And I heard the number of the sealed, 144,000, sealed from every tribe of the sons of Israel.*

The seal of God on these servants is placed on the forehead, signifying their continual consciousness and unbroken communion and communication with the Lord. God will ever be at the forefront of their minds, and they are totally devoted to Him alone.

The number 144,000 is symbolic rather than literal. The number 144 signifies a Spirit guided life. This is supported by the seal upon their thoughts, as we just discussed. One thousand is symbolic of a multiplier to indicate fullness. It also signifies maturity, full stature, mature service, mature judgment, and the glory of God. This number then represents a company of servants who are fully mature and radically obedient to the direction of the Spirit of God, and are therefore qualified and equipped to execute God's judgments as they carry a massive weight of God's glory in an unusual way. So, the figure 144,000 is indicative of the character and calling of these servants, not their number.

These people are of the tribes of the son's of Israel. While I believe that many of them will be believing Jews, I don't think the ranks of this group are limited to Jews. Israel is used symbolically of Christians, both Jew and Gentile, as well as in reference to the nation of Israel, throughout Scripture. These are the *sons* of Israel. The Gentile church is the offspring of Israel, just as believing Jews are.

A few verses later in Rev. 7, John describes a great multitude in heaven.

*Rev 7:9*
*After this I looked, and behold, a great multitude that no one could number, from every nation, from all tribes and peoples and languages, standing before the throne and before the Lamb, clothed in white robes, with palm branches in their hands,*

This multitude is from every people group. Since John was shown this throng immediately after seeing the 144,000, I think it is probable that the two multitudes are actually the same folks, represented differently. This group is clearly identified as being from all nations, further supporting that the 144,000 consists of people from many different people groups, rather than just Jews.

*Rev 7:13-14*
*Then one of the elders addressed me, saying, "Who are these, clothed in white robes, and from where have they*

*come?" I said to him, "Sir, you know." And he said to me, **"These are the ones coming out of the great tribulation. They have washed their robes and made them white in the blood of the Lamb.***

These are saints who are coming out of the great tribulation. The Greek word for *coming* used here is quite interesting. It is *erchomai*[144], (pronounced ER-kaw-my). It is in the present participle form here, which indicates a present continuous action. So, these saints are continuing to come out of the Tribulation, one at a time, as John witnesses this. These are not folks who have all come out at once or at some time in the past. They are showing up amongst the multitude in heaven as they are being martyred, or otherwise killed on earth.[145] We will be looking at this Greek word again when we consider the nature of the Lord's coming a little later.

In one of my personal encounters with the Lord in the heavenly realms, I saw a being of incredible light, gracefully fly about before me. Only the Lord's brilliance was greater than the beautiful light that radiated from the creature in this vision. As it came close to me I could make out a human form within the intense brightness. I asked the Lord who or what this was, and received this answer:

> **"What you see is one of My martyrs. This precious saint sacrificed all out of devotion and love for Me. Precious in My sight is the death of My saints, and precious shall they remain for all eternity. Martyrs wear an extraordinary measure and quality of glory, reserved for them alone. Their great beauty and the ecstatic joy we enjoy, from wearing My glory in such a way, is a testimony to Our faithfulness, one to another. I am with My martyrs at the time of their death in a way unlike anything else one experiences while in their natural body. As these servants of Mine have learned to seek My glory above all else, it is then present with**

---

[144] Strong's NT:2064 This is the transliteration of the lexical form of the word. The form used here is ερχόμενοίς.

[145] The martyrs of Jesus who die during the 3 ½ year Tribulation are also mentioned in Rev 6:9-11, Rev 17:6, Rev 18:24, Rev 20:4

**them in abundance at their passing. Fear is consumed by the fiery cloud of My glory that envelopes them in the moments before they arrive here. They scarcely perceive the moment of their death, as the glory opens the heavens and carries them into My immediate presence. My love and grace are sufficient; stronger than death, stronger than the grave."**

Chapter 11 of Revelation also contains some very interesting things related to the carriers of God's glory during the Tribulation.

*Rev 10:11*
*And I was told, "You must again **prophesy about many peoples and nations and languages and kings."***

It is important to note that in the last verse of Revelation chapter 10, John is told that what he is about to prophesy next has to do with many peoples, nations and kings. So, what comes next, in chapter 11, will be referring to a large number of people rather than just a few.

*Rev 11:1-2*
*Then I was given a measuring rod like a staff, and I was told, "Rise and measure the temple of God and the altar and those who worship there, but do not measure the court outside the temple; leave that out, for it is given over to the nations, and they will trample the holy city for forty-two months.*

John is told to measure the temple of God, the altar and all who worship there. The Lord will at some point take roll call of all who worship Him in Spirit and in truth and seal them with the mark of His ownership. Measuring the altar speaks of judging the quality of the sacrifices and level of obedience in giving up all that the Lord has called His servants to lay down.

Those who have been lax in their worship and preparation before God will be given over to the world to come under the same judgment and wrath as those outside of His household. The time of this judgment upon the nations is to be forty-two months, which is significant, as we will see.

I see this as the fulfillment of the warning Jesus gives earlier in Rev. 3:16 to those that are lukewarm. They are *"spit"* out of the mouth of the Lord to be trampled by the world, the forces of evil and the judgments of God to come. Jesus issued the same warning in Mt. 5:13, and in Mt 25:10-13 (more on this a bit later). You really want to be in the inner chambers of the "temple" before this happens. We covered the way to get into the holy of holies, where the glory dwells, in chapter twelve of this book.

> *Rev 11:3-4*
> *"And I will grant authority to my two witnesses, and they will prophesy for 1,260 days, clothed in sackcloth." These are the two olive trees and the two lampstands that stand before the Lord of the earth.*

Two is the number of witnesses required to bring a charge or accusation against those who would come under judgment.[146] Two also signifies agreement and true testimony. We will see momentarily, that the nature of the prophecy and ministry of these two witnesses is to bring charges against mankind and release the judgments of God against those now locked out of the temple of God. These prophets are backed by an unusual measure of God's authority.

The wearing of sackcloth, or humble garments, is a sign to the people that a prophet is sent to. It is a "visual aid" that signifies the urgent message for those being prophesied over to humble themselves and repent, for the judgment of God is imminent. The simple garments also represent the humility of the prophets, qualifying them to deliver the oracles of divine judgment.

These two witnesses will prophesy for the same period of time that the nations will be judged, as seen in verse 2. This three and a half year period is also mentioned in Daniel 7:25 in reference to the length of the Antichrist's reign, and in Daniel 12:7 as the length of the Tribulation. In Rev 12:14 the same language is used *(for a time,*

---

[146] Dt 17:6, 19:15  Mt 18:16, 26:60  2 Cor 13:1  1 Tim 5:19  Heb 10:28

*and times, and half a time)* in regards to the period of time that the woman (church) is taken into the wilderness to be sustained by God.

The three different ways of describing this period of time[147] are used to stress that the numbers should be taken literally, rather than symbolically. So, these things coincide and will occur over the same 42 month period.

One of the most helpful principles to use in interpreting apocalyptic literature (like Revelation) is to maintain the consistency of the symbols used throughout the book. Once the meaning of a symbol is defined, it is likely to carry that same meaning where it appears throughout the writing. If a particular symbol is not clearly defined within the book where it appears, then we should consider how the symbol is used in other contexts in the Bible.

The two witnesses described here are not two individual people, but a larger company of prophets. There are several indications of this.

John is told that the two witnesses are two olive trees and two lampstands that stand before the Lord of the earth. This is a direct reference to Zechariah 4:2-7. The way this passage ties in with John's vision, and many of the things we have explored in this book, is amazing to me. To begin to see this let's consider how these symbols are used in other places.

John saw Jesus in the midst of seven golden lampstands in Rev. 1:12. The Lord explained to John that the lampstands are the seven churches in Rev 1:20. The number seven signifies completion, the fullness or the totality of a thing. Seven is seen throughout the book of Revelation. So, the lampstands that John saw in Rev.1 and Rev 11 represent the whole, or complete church, with the Lord in its midst. We are to be a light unto the world and bear the presence and testimony of Jesus.

The seven lamps also represent the seven-fold Spirit of God, which John saw during his throne room encounter in Rev 4:5. As we saw at the beginning of chapter eleven of this book, these qualities of the Spirit of the Lord will be an integral part of the lives of these end-time prophets.[148]

---

[147] 42 months, 1260 days, "times, time, and half a time" = 3 ½ years
[148] Isa 11:2-3

Olive trees are not mentioned elsewhere in the book of Revelation. However, Paul uses this symbol to represent the household of God, both Jewish and Gentile believers, in Romans chapter 11. The symbolism of branches is also used in Ezekiel 37:15:22, where the Lord prophesies the restoration and union of all Israel[149] under His rule.

So, the identities of these two witnesses are a company of extraordinary prophets that will be made up of Jewish and Gentile Christians, working in unity to proclaim the oracles of God with great power and authority during the Great Tribulation period at the end of the age. I believe that these *"witnesses"* are likely the same group of people seen in Revelation chapter 7 – the 144,000 we looked at a little earlier.

> *Rev 11:5-6*
> *And if anyone would harm them,* ***fire pours from their mouth and consumes their foes.*** *If anyone would harm them, this is how he is doomed to be killed. They have the power to shut the sky, that no rain may fall during the days of their prophesying, and they have power over the waters to turn them into blood and to strike the earth with every kind of plague, as often as they desire.*

It will be a dreadful thing for those who oppose these prophets of the Lord. The fire that comes from their mouths is the fearfully empowered words they speak. Their preaching and prophesying will be unlike anything heard on earth, up to that time. They will be given the authority to release the terrible judgments of God upon the earth by their words.

The ark is seen in the temple of God at the end of Revelation 11, after John sees the two witnesses resurrected and taken up into heaven.

---

[149] This includes both the lost tribe of Ephraim (Gentiles); and the twelve sons of Israel (Jews).

> *Rev 11:19*
> *Then God's temple in heaven was opened, and the ark of his covenant was seen within his temple. There were flashes of lightning, rumblings, peals of thunder, an earthquake, and heavy hail.*

This is further evidence that the two witnesses are the "arks" of God; the forerunners that are chosen to be carriers of glory; that we considered in chapter 13 of this book. They will be emptied of self and refined in the trials they endure, so as to be entrusted with such awesome power and authority.

Revelation 11 describes some of the greater works that Jesus spoke of that would be done by those who learn to walk in this level of absolute obedience.[150] These prophet's words, thoughts, and deeds will be in absolute submission to God's Spirit. They will have learned to walk as Jesus did while on earth; doing only what they see the Father doing, and saying only what they hear Him saying.[151]

The plagues and various judgments listed in Rev. 11:6 are characteristics of the prophetic ministries of Moses and Elijah. This depicts the purpose and spirit that will be on these prophets. These folks are the ultimate embodiment of what Malachi prophesied.

> *Mal 4:4-6*
> *"Remember the law of my **servant Moses**, the statutes and rules that I commanded him at Horeb for all Israel.*
> *"Behold, **I will send you Elijah the prophet before the great and awesome day of the LORD comes**. And he will turn the hearts of fathers to their children and the hearts of children to their fathers, **lest I come and strike the land with a decree of utter destruction.**"*

Moses typifies the prophet who desires to see the glory of God at any cost. Moses delivered the mandates of God to the people and led them toward the promise. Elijah was the prophet

---

[150] Jn 14:12
[151] Jn 5:19-20

of fire. He challenged Jezebel and the false prophets of his day. Elijah was taken into heaven on a flaming chariot of glory. These will be a few of the earmarks of the prophets seen here in Rev. 11:7 as well.

*And when they have finished their testimony, the beast that rises from the bottomless pit will make war on them and conquer them and kill them,*

Daniel was also told of the power given the Antichrist to kill the saints of God during this three and a half year period.[152] The devil never really develops new tactics. Just as with Moses, Elijah, John the Baptist, Jesus and many other chosen vessels of God, Satan tries to kill them, believing this will thwart God's plans. In reality, this has always backfired on the evil one, just as it will in the end.[153]

So, we see that the chosen of God will walk in great power and authority as they are given an extraordinary endowment of the glory. As stated in chapter thirteen of this book, not all Christians will be entrusted with such ministries of immense power and consequence.

However, we will all have the opportunity to enter into the glory while on earth, and have the glory of God seen in us by the world.[154] To see the nature and timing of this glorious expression of Christ in His church at the end of this age, we'll now go back to Matthew 24.

We can clearly see that the church, or saints of God, will be on earth during the time of tribulation just prior to the return of Christ, in many places in the Bible. The saints of God will be persecuted and will be here during the reign of the Antichrist.[155] The most straight-forward and clear meanings of these texts (and many others) have to be twisted, ignored or otherwise mishandled to try to "prove" that Christians are going to bolt out of here through some imaginary escape hatch before the time of great trouble.

---

[152] Dan 7:21-23
[153] Rev. 19 & 20
[154] 2 Thes 1:5-11
[155] Dan 7:17-28, Dan 8:24-27, Mt 24:9,15-22, 29-31, 2 Thes 2:1-11, Rev 7:9-14, Rev 12:17

We do know that we will be changed and take on an immortal body, at some point.[156] So, the question is when will this event take place and what is the nature of it? Before we can fully understand the answers to this question, we must consider certain events that will take place prior to Christ's return, and the nature and timing of His coming. The "rapture" and the second advent of Jesus are linked in ways many have not yet seen.

Jesus gave us clear warnings about being deceived concerning His return and maintaining a high level of spiritual preparation in Matthew 24 and 25. Earlier in chapter five of this book, we considered the parable of the ten virgins of Matthew 25, and how it depicts our need to stay filled with the oil of the Holy Spirit. What I did not mention there was that Jesus told this parable as part of His response to the question about what signs there would be *before* His second coming and the end of the age. Immediately after describing these signs in Matthew 24, He transitions into two parables concerning preparedness for His return. Some years ago, the Lord spoke to me very clearly concerning all of this, and said:

*"Just as those of My household who studied the Scriptures, and presumed to know the nature of My first coming, failed to perceive it and rejected Me when I arrived, so shall it be at My second coming. They did not know Me in truth, and therefore did not recognize Me in reality."*

Clearly, the message hear is that we must come to know the Lord as well as we possibly can, at all costs, if we are to perceive Him accurately and stand ready at His coming. By now, it should be plain that the ultimate and highest way of coming to know Him is in the realms of glory. So, this should motivate us to press into the Kingdom of God with absolute abandon and fervently cry out for His glory.

As we have progressed through this book, we have seen that maintaining a disciplined, Spirit filled and Spirit led life are crucial. Not only for our normal development in the Kingdom, but as ongoing preparation for ever greater realms of glory. This will all

---

[156] 1 Cor 15:51-54, 1 Thes 4:16-18

become even more imperative as we approach the coming of the Lord.

Jesus talked in parables and used metaphors to conceal the mysteries He spoke of. Not to frustrate, but to test the heart of the hearer. Our Lord loves a good puzzle. He reveals things to those who seek Him diligently for truth, and in the proper time. Keeping these things in mind will help as we go through the rest of this chapter.

I will be making reference to specific verses and words in Matthew 24 and will be jumping around a bit. So, it would be a good idea to use your Bible along side this book while you read through this section, to help in following through these concepts.

After pronouncing judgment on the religious leaders and Jerusalem in Matthew 23 Jesus went up to the Mount of Olives and predicted the destruction of the temple. Many of the events the Lord predicted came to pass during the fall of Jerusalem in 70 A.D., as well as many of the things He prophesied in chapter 24. However, at the time of this writing, these prophesies have not been ultimately fulfilled.

There is a hermeneutical principle (rule for interpreting Scripture) called the Law of Multiple Reference. It basically states that a passage of Scripture may apply to multiple events that occur at different times. This is especially common in the prophetic writings of the Bible. A prophecy may find partial fulfillment at one time and yet find its fullest ultimate fulfillment some time after the first.[157] So, much of what the Lord spoke about in Matthew 24 and 25 is yet to be completely fulfilled.

Jesus is asked by His disciples when the things He prophesied would take place, and what would be the signs of His *coming*, and the end of the age. The word used in verse 3 for "*coming*" is *parousia* [158] (pronounced *paw-roo-SEE-uh*). It means the physical arrival of someone. This is very important to the rest of our examination of this passage. The disciples did not have any concept of the Lord's coming in the spiritual sense, by way of the indwelling Holy Spirit at that time. So, they were

---

[157] Examples of this are Mal 4:5-6, Joel 2:28-32
[158] Strong's NT:3952 This is the transliteration of the lexical form of the word. The form used here is παρουσίας

asking about the signs of the Lord's physical return. The word *parousia* is used throughout the New Testament to signify the physical arrival of someone.[159]

In Mt 24:4 the Lord starts out His answer to these questions by warning them not to be led astray by those who would come claiming to be Him. He warns of this again later in verses 11, and 23-26. In order to interpret this passage correctly, we first need to recognize that the Lord is not describing these things in chronological order all the way through. In places, He is referencing a time and events that He has already mentioned previously.

Jesus uses the word *parousia* in verse 27 to describe His coming as being like the flashing of lightning from the east to the west. He is referring to His physical return to earth here.

However, in verse 30 the Lord does not use the word *parousia* where we see the word *"coming"*, but He uses the word *erchomai*[160], (pronounced ER-kaw-my). This is the same word used in Rev 7:14 to describe the coming out of the Tribulation of the martyred saints that we considered earlier in this chapter. It indicates a gradual and continuing process, rather than a one time event. Jesus also used this word (*erchomai*) when He spoke to His disciples about His *coming* to them by way of the Holy Spirit in John's gospel.[161] It is also the same word used in the parallel passages of this account of Mt 24 in the other synoptic Gospels.[162]

So, the Lord is describing His second advent, or physical coming, when He uses the word *parousia,* and He is referring to something else when He uses the word *erchomai.* He is actually describing His coming in a spiritual sense as being the lead-in to His physical appearing. Jesus is describing the arrival and outpouring of His Spirit on earth and upon His *"elect"* in a gradual way that escalates in intensity and power, culminating in His sudden physical

---

[159] 1 Cor 16:17, Phil 1:6,
[160] Strong's NT:2064 This is the transliteration of the lexical form of the word. The form used here is ερχόμενον

[161] Jn 14:18, 14:28, 15:26, 16:7, 16:28,
[162] Mk 14:26, Lk 21:27

return to earth. Let's take a closer look at some key passages to see how this fits together.

> *Matt 24:30-31*
> *Then will appear **in heaven the sign of the Son of Man**, and then all the tribes of the earth will mourn, and they will see the Son of Man coming on the **clouds of** heaven with power and **great glory**. And he will send out his angels with a loud trumpet call, and they will gather his elect from the four winds, from one end of heaven to the other.*

The Greek word used for *then* at the beginning of verse 30, when considered within the context of this passage, does not indicate that what follows occurs after the events described in the previous verses, but at about the same time as those events. Notice Jesus said the *"sign of the Son of Man"* would appear in heaven. The Greek word used for heaven[163] can also mean sky, atmosphere or air. Also, note that He said that His *sign* would appear, not His body or person. The word used for *sign*[164] means miracle, token or wonder. Next He says that all the tribes of the earth will see Him *coming (erchomai)* on the clouds of heaven. This is the fulfillment of the prophecy the angels made at His ascension.[165]

If Jesus was referring to His second advent, how would it be possible for all people to see Him coming out of the sky at once? His second coming *(parousia)* will be sudden and localized as He descends onto the Mount of Olives.[166] Here, the Lord says He will be coming *(erchomai)* in clouds of power and great glory. So, all will see His coming *(erchomai)* because He is speaking about the display of His glory through His Body in the earth.

I see this as describing His coming in clouds of glory for His saints to be enveloped, empowered and filled to then reveal Him to all the tribes of the earth, in the ways we have seen earlier. This also depicts His *parousia,* as mentioned in Mt 24:27, being the climax to the events He describes throughout this chapter.

---

[163] Strong's NT:3772   ουρανός ouranos (oo-ran-os')
[164] Strong's NT:4592  σημεῖον semeion (say-mi'-on)
[165] Acts 1:9-11
[166] Zech 14:4

Further evidence of this is seen as we read on. The Lord says that no one knows the day or hour of His *erchomai* in verse 36 because what He just described is not a single event. It is His glorious appearing in the saints over a period of time.

In verses 37-39 He says that these things will happen just as in the days of Noah. This is another piece of the puzzle that indicates a period of time before His *parousia* when He will be coming (*erchomai*) in glory over a period of time. Noah was told to get into the ark seven days before the rain came and the waters under the earth burst forth. This corresponds to the seven year Tribulation period.[167] God is calling us to get into the ark of His glory.

In Mt 24:42-44 Jesus urges us to remain awake as He is coming as a thief in the night. This same expression is used elsewhere in reference to His coming (*erchomai*).[168] This does not mean *suddenly* or without warning, as many have thought. This is often taken to support His coming (*parousia*) as being instantaneous and by complete surprise. While His *parousia* will come suddenly and as a complete surprise to many, it will not be so for those who watch and wait faithfully, and take on more of the glory, like the five wise virgins.

A thief does not come in a flash and make His presence known to everyone. A thief comes in quietly through a way and at a time that is unexpected. Thus the Lord's repeated warnings about not being deceived and staying awake and prepared spiritually. The parable of the ten virgins[169] we discussed earlier is an even more direct way of showing us that it is the filling with the Spirit and power of God, and the glory that will shine from us as light, that is the fuel that keeps us in a ready condition.

Not only is the glory the grace that will be bestowed upon us to persevere in these times of trouble and execute the works God calls us to, it is the very thing that will translate us from this realm into eternity. It is the fuel that will change our mortal bodies into their immortal, incorruptible state, at the resurrection. The cloud of glory

---

[167] The Tribulation is thought to be 7 years long as seen in a number of places in scripture (Dan 9:24-27). The "Great Tribulation" is the last 3 ½ year period of the seven.
[168] Lk 12:39, 1 Thes 5:2-4, 2 Pet 3:10
[169] Mt 24:1-13

is the substance of what we will need to be changed when the *parousia* does come. Just like Enoch, Elijah, and Jesus, those who are alive at the time of His *parousia*, will be transformed into their resurrection bodies by the glory they have come to abide in. The final transformation will happen in an instant, but the fuel needed to make it happen will be poured out over a period of time.

The time to prepare for all of this is now. Those who think they can jump onboard when they see things start to get tough, or perceive the things the Lord warned about, will have waited too long to start the process, just like the five foolish virgins.

For those who prepare, endure and overcome there awaits an eternal reward of the most magnificent glory, to be enjoyed forever. Let us press on and finish well, that we might be found ready at the Lord's appearing.[170] My prayer is that you will be found faithful and full of the life, likeness and glory of our wonderful Lord in that day.

**Activation**

*Lord, please help me to be watchful and diligent in seeking to be filled continually with Your Spirit. Cover me in Your glory and help me to be found faithful in obedience to all You will require of me in preparing the way for Your glorious appearing. Make me fit for service in the drama of the ages and let me be one who shows forth Your glory as a testimony to Your majesty and goodness. I desire to make Your glory known in the earth and be found full of Your likeness, presence and glory at Your coming. Come Lord Jesus! Amen.*

---

[170] 2 Tim 4:6-8

# Ω
## §
# Conclusion

The more of the glory we acquire in the these days, the more of the glory we will be able to endure and minister out of when the Lord begins to pour it out in progressively increasing measure. As we become drenched and changed by the glory, our capacity for more increases. This process then escalates until we take on more of the substance of the glory realm than the natural realm. Ultimately, we then pass from this world into the realms of glory, as pure, incorruptible immortality displaces mortality, where we will forever be with the Lord of Glory.

Many prophetic words and teachings have gone forth proclaiming the great things that have been prepared for those who believe and obey. While we can expect to enter into a measure of some of these promises before Christ's physical return to Earth, I think that much of what He is now speaking to us will not manifest in fullness until He establishes His physical reign on earth. Much of the prophecy going forth concerning wealth, honor, ruling and reigning, and the kind, are not likely to come to pass in fullness this side of the Millennial reign of Christ.

I believe that the Lord is speaking these things to us now to give us hope and encouragement to press through the tough times that are ahead. They are true words of destiny, but as is our way many times, we presume that what He speaks will come to pass when most convenient for us. It is a common pattern for humans to misunderstand the nature of prophecy until it comes to pass.

The way to enter into our promises is to enter into the glory. Now. Make Him your passion and He will be your portion. The promise of endless joy, cloaked in His essence and ever coming to know His marvelous Person for all eternity, is of greater value than anything else[171].

*Rev 21:3*
*And I heard a loud voice from the throne saying, "Behold, the dwelling place of God is with man. He will dwell with them, and they will be his people, and God himself will be with them as their God.*

*Rev 21:22*
*And I saw no temple in the city, for its temple is the Lord God the Almighty and the Lamb.*

God will be our dwelling place and we will be His. Even now, He is reconciling all things unto Himself. For those who desire Him above all else, who purify themselves in obedience, and endure the fires of affliction, complete union with God in the realms of His glory will be their eternal reward. This is the culmination of a great mystery. This is our destiny.

---

[171] Mt 6:19-21, Mt 13:44-46

# About the Author

Kevin Paul Stephen has earned the degrees of Master of Divinity, Master of Theology, and Bachelor of Theology from *Christian Life School of Theology*. However, that is not what qualifies him to write this book.

*Acts 4:13*
*Now when they saw the boldness of Peter and John, and perceived that they were uneducated, common men, they were astonished. And they recognized that they had been with Jesus.*

While theological training and study are of great benefit in becoming a fit minister in God's Kingdom, being with Jesus is the one thing that qualifies anyone to speak on His behalf. Out of a growing and intimate relationship with the Lord of Glory come the preparation and anointing to carry out His will. Kevin has been with Jesus, and this book is a product of that relationship.

Kevin lives "outside the box", in many respects, as he ministers where the Lord sends him. God regularly takes Kevin to various places in Canada, Hawaii and within the continental United States to break open spiritual territory and make prophetic declarations over specific areas and people. Supernatural experiences in the heavenly realms often occur during these underground missions for God. Kevin also carries a burden for the United Kingdom, the islands of the South Pacific and Asia.

Kevin can be contacted at:
kevin@brokenbreadministries.org

Visit the web site of Broken Bread Ministries to read Kevin's prophetic writings, or to subscribe to the ministry's free newsletter and to automatically receive new prophecies as they are released at:
www.brokenbreadministries.org

To order additional copies of
# Realms of Glory
*Encountering God in the Last Days*

Visit us online at:
## www.brokenbreadpublishing.com

Printed in the United States
91156LV00013B/10/A